To my prized friend, Together we will make the name Lott, Guax!

Lott
♡ Love
Sam

Degreed & Homeless

By: Tamarcus Lott

Copyright © 2020

All rights reserved. No part of this publication may be reproduced, distributed, or transmitted in any form by any means, including photocopying, recording, or other electronic or mechanical methods without the prior written permission of the publisher, except in the case of brief quotations embodied in critical reviews and certain other noncommercial uses permitted by copyright law. For permission requests, write to the publisher addressed "Attention: Permissions Coordinator," at the address below.

ISBN: 9798609563637 (Paperback)

ISBN: (Hardcover)

Any references to historical events, real people, or real places are used fictitiously. Names, characters, and places are products of the author's imagination.

Front cover image by: Kimani McCullough

Book design by: Tamarcus Lott

Printed by: Kindle Direct Publishing, Barnes and Nobel Press

To Kalyn and Bria

Without you both, I wouldn't have made it through the story that lies within these pages. As a small token of love, I dedicate this book to you both, my Queens.

Thank you

Table of Contents

Preface 1

Degreed & Homeless

DEGREED

CHAPTER 1 *Degreed* 12
CHAPTER 2 *Decisions* 21
CHAPTER 3 *Senior Banquet* 30
CHAPTER 4 *May 2017* 36
CHAPTER 5 *Oath Of Enlistment* 38
CHAPTER 6 *Basic Combat Training* 39
CHAPTER 7 *December 2017* 61
CHAPTER 8 *Sierra Vista* 66
CHAPTER 9 *February* 71
CHAPTER 10 *Conformity* 76
CHAPTER 11 *Depression* 80
CHAPTER 12 *90 Days* 86
CHAPTER 13 *Self Realization* 91
CHAPTER 14 *March* 95
CHAPTER 15 *Mental Evaluation* 98
CHAPTER 16 *May* 103

HOMELESS

CHAPTER 17 *New Apartment* 108
CHAPTER 18 *New me, New Job, Who dis?* 111
CHAPTER 19 *May 15, 2019* 114
CHAPTER 20 *July 2018* 119

CHAPTER 21 *Homeless* 123
CHAPTER 22 *Distraction* 129
CHAPTER 23 *September* 136
CHAPTER 24 *Lord, Why me?* 140
CHAPTER 25 *Resentment* 149
CHAPTER 26 *All the way home* 151
CHAPTER 27 *What now?* 154
CHAPTER 28 *Make New Mistakes* 157

Preface

I believe the best thing, and the worst thing, my mom ever told me was, "You can be anything in this world if you put your mind to it."

Hearing those words, understanding those words, opened my mind to an endless world of possibilities. Without a shadow of a doubt, I knew I could become whatever I wanted to be. I dreamt about those words, "anything I wanted to be." Anything?

I became obsessed with my future aspirations and grew impatient with the present. I desperately needed to know what I was going to be when I grew up. I needed to know what type of life I would live, what type of car I would drive, and if I would be socially active within my community. Or was I going to live paycheck to paycheck, worrying about bills and where I was going to get my next meal?

A lot of children live blindly to the real world, which is typically how it's supposed to be. When you're young, you don't have to worry about the stresses of life-it's the ultimate pro of being a child. But this was not the case for me. I was constantly poking my nose into business that didn't concern me. I wanted to know how much my mom made in her job. I wanted to know how much her bills were to the exact dollar. I wanted to understand how to be an adult.

But, despite my best efforts my mom was able to shelter us from the real world. It was always, "Wait until you're eighteen and out on your own." But my eighteenth birthday seemed like it would never come. I struggled with being a child. Nothing about childhood gave me any satisfaction, because once we all turned eighteen, everything in my childhood no longer mattered. I couldn't wait until my eighteenth birthday to start experiencing real life things. My mom gave me excellent advice and scenarios pertaining to real life, but she never told us about her own personal experiences. All of my siblings, including myself, always guessed about who she was or what it was like for her growing up. She didn't share stories with us, which is a hint about how she got in trouble or how she had my older brother at such an early age. These things intrigued me because here she was now, a fully functional adult with children and an ok paying job. But there was no storyline I could piece together as to how she got here, which could help me once I made it out on my own.

This made me particularly nosy. I eavesdropped on my mom's conversations, butted in when people weren't talking to me, and concerned myself with things that had nothing to do with me. At family gatherings, I avoided going outside to play with my cousins in order to stay in the house with the adults, hoping I would hear them talking about stuff they would never say around us kids. I made it my business to be in other people's business. It wasn't so I could go back and tell anyone what I heard but it was because they talked about things that I knew nothing about. I was never interested in the things kids my age talked about. What adults did in their day-to-day lives was far more interesting than playground chat.

I was intrigued by their conversations, their lives, and their thoughts. Every time my mom had company, my brother and I would come out of our rooms to greet them, but once they started talking, we were quickly dismissed to our rooms. I can vividly remember every time my older cousin, "Pop," would come over. They always gossiped about the juiciest things going on at work, about family, and friends. My feelings would instantly be crushed because I couldn't sit and listen in on the latest adult news. Despite being sent off to my room, I'd purposely leave my door cracked just enough for me to be able to hear what they were conversing about. The more I listened, the more I started to learn. I was fully aware that there were some things kids my age had no business hearing but I liked what I heard, no matter what it was.

I felt strange knowing I could keep up with adult conversations but not be able to chime in when something crossed my mind. I always felt different than others my age, I knew I didn't think like them, nor did I act like them. I figured I thought like other adults because my thoughts were more serious and my interests were focused on more things that adults worried about, such as paying bills, the evening news, politics, or life on the job. It seemed unfair to me that adults censored their lives whenever children were around. They made it seem as if they lived in a secret world behind a door that said "No Children Allowed" in big bold red letters. I desperately wanted to know what went on behind that door, and couldn't wait until the day when I was old enough to know what went on in the "adult world." I figured someday day I'd be eighteen and living as an adult, just like them, so I thought I should know what it was like to be one before I was one.

Paying close attention to those older than I molded the way I behaved. I was often told that I was very mature for my age. My mom knew it and I knew it. I learned that with maturity comes wisdom. I might have not been as wise as I thought I was but I was definitely smarter than most; I brought home A's and B's every report card. I read way ahead of my grade level and came in second place during a school-wide spelling bee in the eighth grade. I was smart and loved learning. Oddly enough, school was the only place where I didn't feel like a child. My wit and maturity allowed me to hold conversations with teachers like I never could at home or with other family members. I wanted to always be around those that were older than me. There were countless times when I was silenced by an adult or reprimanded for something I said. It bothered me deeply to be made to feel small because of my age because my mind was far more advanced than they could believe. Even at home my mom and I would constantly bump heads and she steadily reminded me to "stay in a child's place." It was very rare in my family for children to sit amongst adults while they were talking. There were only few times I was lucky enough to stay so quiet the adults would forget I was in the room, but I always gave myself away just as the conversation would get really deep or extra juicy. I could never stop myself from chiming in on or laughing or humming "mmhm" in agreement.

I think differently, I've always known that about myself. I didn't want to be your friend if you didn't have anything of value to talk about. Clothes, cars, shoes, video games weren't subjects in which I was interested. I wanted to talk about politics, homework, history, and my future. But this made me a very boring person to other kid. In fact, I only had one real friend who shared the same interests as me. Instead of making friends by commonalities, I started making friends in school by making people laugh. It was odd to talk about how much I wanted to be a successful doctor, or how I wanted to cure asthma. Because at the time that's what interested me, pulmonology. Nobody knew what a pulmonologist was or what they did, not even my mom. Most of my childhood could be summed up in two words, doctors and hospitals. I suffered severely from asthma. I couldn't play sports, I couldn't go to recess during the spring and, once it got to cold, I couldn't go outside to play in the neighborhood. I was prescribed so much medicine I subconsciously started learning about the pulmonary system. So instead of boring people to death about how I wanted to cure a cardiovascular disease, I cracked jokes and talked back to teachers, only because it made the other kids like me.

The older I got the more I became familiar with the charismatic personality I've grown into today. I was almost two different people at home versus at school. At school, I wasn't quite the class clown but I was far from the quietest in the class. My grades were the only things that kept me from looking like a complete fool. I was very silly and had a smart mouth, and I was in constant trouble. Teachers hated how I kept the class off task with my distractions, and they hated it even more when I questioned their authority. The more trouble I caused and the more I made people laugh, the faster I became one of the "popular kids in school." However, in comparison, at home I was very reserved, quiet, and shut away in my room, reading books and watching CNN.

In the early part of my childhood, I lived with all four of my older siblings; my older brother, two older sisters, and my twin brother. My older siblings are all ten plus years older than my twin and me. So, by the start of middle school, my siblings were grown and out of the house, leaving just my brother and me in the house with our mom. Although I have a twin brother, we look and act nothing like twins. He's always been taller and had more weight than me. We share some of the same facial features and have some similarities about our personalities, but overall, we're like night and day. I was the nerd and he was the jock. We both were pretty popular throughout school but we never had the same group of friends. I knew of everyone in our school, my jokes for everyone. I loved making any and everybody smile and laugh. But, no one knew me personally except the one or two people I confided in up until high school one of the being my best friend, Kalyn. She's basically the female version of me. Idk how we met but we met in middle school, probably doing something ridiculously goofy.

My brother hung out with the athletes and neighborhood delinquents, and he is far goofier than me. He preferred to stay outside and play football and basketball with the kids around the neighborhood after school. Our elementary, middle, and high school were performing arts schools. I was on the honors program and the performing arts program. I sang in the choir and was active in a bunch of student organizations. Seemingly living two different lives while at school, we didn't have much to talk about at home. Despite being so different, we were still close. There was an unspoken bond between us; we stuck up for each other and had each other's back whenever times got rough.

Life felt simple and easy growing up. My mom kept my brother and me sheltered away from a lot of things. We spent the majority of our free time in church. My mom, to this day, is super religious. I joke with my friends by calling her "Jesus's sister." My brother and I didn't experience much outside of church and family. My parents divorced a few years after my brother and I were born. My mom voiced how she wanted to keep a close relationship with our dad's side of the family. She kept his name to keep us from having different last names than her. Although they were divorced, we spent most major holidays celebrating with my dad's side of the family. We never questioned it because we always loved being with them. They knew how to come together and have a good time, no matter the occasion, and they continued to embrace my mom even through their breakup.

    I remember pulling up at my aunt and uncle's house only to open the doors to the car and hear the thunderous laughter coming from inside the house. The vibes were much different whenever we opted to spend time with my mom's side of the family. My older cousins, aunts and uncles, even my mom made it seem like a chore to attend family gatherings. Nobody ever acted like they wanted to be there. They all seemed like they secretly hated one another. The house was always quiet and the adults usually watched TV, avoiding any real conversation with one another. My mom always used my brother and me as scapegoats to leave early. She'd ask us if we were ready to go in front of everyone, knowing we'd say yes in unison without hesitation. We knew the drill whenever we visited mom's side of the family we were in quick and out quicker. It was great for her and even better for us. My brother and I hated spending Christmas with her side of the family because it meant Christmas would be gloomy and boring. We mainly spent the holidays with my fathers side of the family. Often we'd drive over my mom's sister's house or visit her mother after we spent most of the day somewhere else. It wasn't until we experienced a tragic death on my father's side of the family that disrupted cherished family traditions. My cousin's death caused a lot of divide in my family, forcing me to figure out why my mom's side was so dysfunctional? What happened to them? How was it that I my father and his family was so loving and had a great sense of togetherness and humor, whereas the other side of my family seemed battered, torn, and falling apart. It was never said, but it was obvious my mom was torn between a divorced functioning family and a dysfunctional family of her own. One side seemed to have all the love and cohesion a family needed, while the other side had always been divided and complacent. I never knew why my mom's side of the family operated the way that they did, but with growing curiosity, I sought to find out.

My mom raised all five of her children as a single mother. You would expect all of us to be close to our mother, being that she single-handedly raised us. Instead, we all have our reservations as to how we were raised. No relationship with a parent and their child is perfect, but our relationship with our mom isn't even close. Listening to my older siblings' stories about their childhood, and considering whatever my mom was going through before my brother and I were born, we had it much easier than them.

My mom had my oldest brother around fifteen and my two sisters followed a few years behind him. They were raised at a time when my mom was still young and learning how to manage life's obstacles. Still, she provided for them beyond belief. The bills were always paid and food was always in the house. Providing wasn't her shortcoming. Her shortcomings were cycled down from generations through her mother. Her mother didn't teach her life lessons, incoherently passing on another cycle of poor parenting onto yet another generation. It's hard to believe the person my grandma once was. She was absent because of work and men, and at one point, she was on drugs. But, she always paid her bills, had food in the fridge, and clothes for my mom and her three sisters. My mom voiced, overtly, that she wished her mom would've taught her lessons like; *don't have kids at an early age, save your money for the future,* and many other motherly lectures that fell by the wayside. Of course, I wasn't there to see it for myself but, the hurt I've heard my mom and oldest sister express makes me believe every word. Although we know better doesn't mean we'll do better in the future ,as a result, my older brother and two sisters never finished high school. It's unfair to put all the blame on parenting because my sisters and brother did their fair share of dirt, but children are products of their environment. It seemed like the way my mom treated them pushed my older siblings away from her, so they rebelled. My brother and I were too young to understand what was going on at the time. As we got older and started learning about our different family members, we only knew them as being a family member. For instance, I only know my aunt for being my aunt. If they weren't a part of my family, they were near strangers to me because I knew nothing about them. This went for everyone in my mom's family. I knew only as much about them from what my mom told us about them. I never knew how my uncle and aunt met; I knew little to nothing about my siblings themselves, nor their fathers. The intimate personal things one should know about their loved ones, I never knew.

What I did know was that no one had any money, higher education was not a thing, and relationships throughout the family were either nonexistent or holding on by a string; I only had to take a small peek through the window to see why things were the way they were.

The older I got the more I paid attention to these things on both sides of the family. I had to understand the people I came from. I needed to know: would I end up like them? Would I be another generation adding to the cycle of poverty and dearth of a proper education? My sisters and brothers are grown now, and I see what they've become, and I don't like it. They struggle with the real world because they never graduated high school. It's a painful truth to deal with. My siblings weren't the only ones struggling with education—my entire maternal side of the family struggled. No one had any education outside of high school, nor did anyone have a career. The lack of education and financial stability made life a complete struggle for everyone around me. I knew there was more to life than complaining about bills and worrying about affording pampers and milk for my baby. In my years of observing, I realized my family was stuck in a cycle of making the same mistakes. No one knew any better, so no one did any better.

By the end of high school, I knew better but I wasn't sure if I'd do better. Those four years were flooded with fears of living paycheck to paycheck, living on the street, or working a job I hated. All my life my mom, my dad, my grandma, and so many others close to me worked jobs they despised, and I desperately wanted to do better for myself. I knew life offered more than what I was used to, so I became focused. I focused on my academics during my last two years of high school in hopes of going to college. I knew there was no other option; I had to be the first to go to college and bring home a degree. A degree was the only way I'd live differently than my mom and dad and my brothers and sisters. My teachers, principals, and guidance counselors went to great lengths to ensure that college was the next step for all graduates. They painted a vivid picture of life without college, which was a life I was very familiar with. I knew I would get my degree in four years; nothing could've stopped me from being a first-generation graduate.

But what I didn't know was that a year after walking across the stage, I'd lose everything I owned and end up living on the street. I knew I had the mindset to lead me to my dream job and dream life. I begged for adulthood as I grew up, I craved independence and responsibility, and I tried so hard to make new mistakes and stay clear of the path my loved ones went down. Somehow, I ended up in a worse predicament than all of them. This is how I became degreed and homeless.

Degreed & Homeless

Degreed

CHAPTER 1
Degreed

Every morning before school started, just after opening my eyes, I started the day by praying, "God, please let my mom live long enough to see the day I graduate from high school." You'd think that it was strange of me to pray, considering how my mom was never terminally ill, and that she had actually been pretty healthy most of her life. Still, I couldn't help but fear that, somehow, life would be cruel and rob my mom and me from one of the proudest moments of our lives. It would be her first chance to see a child of her own graduate high school. But, with the blessing of having twins, she was able to witness two of her boys walking across the stage for the first time.

I anticipated our graduation for years and couldn't have been more proud to graduate as the class president. I was honored to speak on behalf of my class and introduce the mayor of Memphis as the ceremony speaker. Becoming the class president was by no chance of luck. I intentionally ran for the position because I knew whomever won would speak at graduation. One day I realized my brother and my names would be called right after one another alphabetically, mine following his. The thought of my brother's name being called first never sat well with me. I knew our graduation was a huge gift to my mom, and I wanted my name to be first one she heard. Being class president meant my name would be called after the valedictorian and salutatorian, and therefore, before my brother's. Ultimately, this was a way for my family to have two separate moments to celebrate my brother and me as our names were called and we walked across the stage and headed into our adult lives.

Months before graduation my brother decided to enlist in the Army. I never suspected he would end up joining the military, but I wasn't totally surprised when he did. My brother had always had a fascination with weapons and artillery. He chose to join under the infantry division to learn combat and arms, and to later use those skills to become a police officer. As for me, I was off to college. A few weeks following graduation, I received an acceptance letter to Jackson State University. The only way I can explain how I ended up deciding to go to JSU is that I didn't choose Jackson State, Jackson State chose me.

The moment I found out I was accepted into a college I was surrounded by all of my siblings. I felt a slight weight fall on my shoulders in that very moment. I looked at my brothers and sisters and I thought to myself, "Why me?" No one knew what I was really thinking in the moment. I'm sure everybody believed I was happy to be going to school, but it was unimaginably bigger than just going to school. This was a moment in my family's history when our lives STOPPED repeating themselves. My brother and I stopped the cycle of dropping out of high school, and now it was my turn to stop the cycle of not pursuing a higher education and, hopefully, ending the cycle of poverty as well. As soon as I got the email that I was accepted into school, I knew I would make it to the end and earn my degree. In my eyes, the acceptance letter I held in my hand and the degree I would hold in four years were the same thing.

But how and why was it me that broke the cycle? This was a question that I simply couldn't answer. Nevertheless, I embraced it and vowed to become a first-generation graduate.

Freshman year opened my eyes to an entirely new world I knew nothing about. Jackson State was the only HBCU I applied to—I didn't even know what HBCU meant before freshman orientation. My high school had a majority of black students, but my teachers were mostly white. I was gifted enough be apart of the Creative and Performing Arts program from elementary until high school as well as graduating with honors. The CAPA program and honors program were filled with students whom lived outside distract. In a nutshell, my schooling was pretty diverse. I had very few black teachers, but those few happened to graduate from an HBCU, but that history wasn't taught in my school. The only schools I was familiar with were schools like Harvard, Georgetown, the University of Memphis, and UT Knox. I'd never heard of universities like Howard, Bethune-Cookman, or Jackson State. Had it not been for a college tour my junior year of high school, JSU would've never chosen me to be apart of their institution of higher learning. JSU was on the slate of many colleges and universities on my high school's annual junior's college tour trip. JSU wasn't the most impressive but was far from the least impressive of the schools we visited. At the time of our tour, we were offered to apply with no application fee, not thinking about if I would get accepted or not.

Most of the peers I met during orientation were third-and-fourth-year generation graduates from HBCUs. I didn't have parents to tell me endless stories about their college years, therefore I knew next to nothing about college life. I knew I would have way more freedom than I did at home with my mom. I knew in all the movies college kids got drunk and partied, had a lot of sex, and smoked weed. Before heading off to JSU, I barely ever drank and had never smoked weed in my life.

Also, I knew that football games were the highlight of college life, but no one prepared me for games at a predominantly black college. There is no explanation for the way I felt during my first football game at JSU. I thought I was at a concert and a cookout at the same damn time. For most of the game, I stood in drunken amazement of the band and the crowds of black people all gathered in one place, on one accord.

This experience was a hidden pocket of black culture that I knew nothing about, and it gave me a sense of pride and belonging. Our band, The Sonic Boom of the South, the J Settes, the students, the alumni, the faculty, all made it seem like it was a huge family barbecue, celebrating black excellence. The momentum lasted from the time the game began well into the night at the after-parties. I'm not even sure if our football team lost or won that night, but everybody went home as if we won. The horns from the tubas and the drum line kept the crowd turnt throughout the entire four quarters. Halftime was the same but even more so. Honestly, the entire experience was a high I still can't explain.

My eyes were so wide the entire first semester. I felt beyond excited and ambitious, yet scared all at the same time. Desperately, I wanted to be just as popular in college as I was in high school. Every student organization seemed to have something to offer me, and by joining them all it would be that much easier to get to know people. Many of the college stories my teachers talked about were about their college roommates and how they had been best friends since they met in undergrad. I wanted that. I prayed for a friend, a lifelong friend so I too could tell stories to my children how I met so-and-so way back when. Not knowing I met the first of three life long friends within my first week on campus.

Freshman week was full of events that all freshman thought they wanted to attend. The annual volunteer event was one I thought I wanted to attend. I came dressed to impress but there was real hard labor that need to be done. I finagled my way inside with the air conditioner and stumbled upon Jared. We both mistook the event for a social gathering but when we realized it was the opposite, we were the first to volunteer for the work that needed to be done inside, out of the sun. Being the only two picked to work inside, we reveled in the glory of finessing our way out of working our fingers to the bone and became the best of friends from then on.

My high school teachers ranted and raved on how college work would be so much harder. I thought harder how? Just study and pass the test, simple. Academically, I was arrogant and irresponsible with my coursework. I did so well through grade school, and I thought that it would be easy to excel the same way in college. I had no balance between campus life and academics. While I thrived socially, joined student organizations, and started to travel for the first time with one of the largest organization on campus, I hardly paid attention at all to actually growing as a student.

My first year at JSU made me realize how sheltered I was growing up. I wanted to do everything I couldn't do back home. It wasn't long before I started smoking weed and drinking. In high school, I looked down on people who smoked weed, but in college I was determined to living life to the fullest. I really wanted to get the full college experience because no one else in my family had experienced life on campus.

By the end of the semester, however, I already found myself on academic probation, meaning if my grades didn't improve, I would be kicked out by the end of the next semester. When I returned home I told my mom grades were just like in high school, A's and B's. I avoided showing her my actual grades because she was paying out of her pocket for me to afford my classes. I maxed out on student loans even though I had a partial scholarship, and it still wasn't enough to cover my full tuition. So my mom sacrificed to send me money to eat as well as money for payments on tuition. There was no way I could tell her I was throwing it all away by waiting until college to make D's and F's for the first time in my life.

The return to my dorm was highly anticipated during my break. I missed the freedom of my dorm, my friends on campus, and everything else. I was my own person there. My roommate wasn't the best friend I was going to tell my children about, but we got along well enough. But, I had to reevaluate life over the holiday break. I was going to college to become something different yet I was trying to keep up with the crowd. I wouldn't become a first generation graduate smiling in everyone's faces.

I was in college for one reason: to graduate. Not to make friends. I had to realize friendships would come naturally, but my education was ultimately my reason for being there. I fell back tremendously in my involvement in campus activities. Not just because I knew I had to start focusing on my coursework, but also because I wasn't actually making friends. I was making people laugh and they liked having me around. Nothing was wrong with that, but those people didn't know me, and they only liked me for my witty personality and my snappy jokes. I was trying to make friends with the entire campus of Jackson State. I learned that not everyone is your friend, no matter how much they laugh at your jokes. I thought innocently and was very naive freshman year. In high school I didn't have any "haters." I've always had a charming and easy-going personality. I never thought someone would try to take advantage of someone like me; I never thought people would talk about someone like me behind my back. But they did. And so the popular kid quickly became the quiet, shy guy in the classroom. I realized I wasn't in high school anymore. I wasn't here to make people laugh, I wanted to make real friends, not turn up buddies.

Halfway through my spring semester I finally found a balance. I was still involved around campus, but I purposefully took time out to do homework and to study, rather than to show my face at meetings and talk and socialize with everyone. However, all that effort of setting time out to study was a waste. Studying was never my way of retaining information. I'm a procrastinator at heart. I would learn the material in class and wouldn't freshen up until the morning before the test. Despite this being risky and irresponsible, my grades started to improve, and by the end of the semester I wasn't on academic probation anymore and I could show my mom proof of my actual grades.

Instead of bumming out in Memphis for the summer, I applied for a paid internship, outside my major, just to collect a check. On top getting paid, housing was provided as well. The internship turned out to be a great experience but I gained yet another life long friend, Bria. Bria was an undercover spy the night I met her (insider). The next day, I couldn't find her because she'd let her hair down and put on make up. Eventually, assignments were giving out to all the interns. Bria and I were given the same assignment, at the same location. Bria had a car, I didn't, making her my ride to work everyday. I don't know what possessed me to repeatedly get in the car with Bria because I seriously thought I was gone to die at the expense of her driving. She drives like a bat out of hell but I trusted her with my life, forcing her to become my best friend.

Sophomore year I became even less involved, but was elected for a top position on the executive board for one of the organizations in which I was a part, keeping me more involved on campus than I cared to be. My second year of college was far more difficult than the first year. My mom no longer could afford to send me money to help pay for classes. It was solely up to me to figure out how I was going to put myself through school. I got a job off-campus as well as a work-study job on campus. I was always in and out of focus with my academics because of work. I struggled trying to prioritize the two. Which was more important, work or school? I needed to work to pay for school, but I needed time to do homework so I didn't fail my classes. All my money was going towards school and I almost never had money for myself. No one told me that being broke and struggling was a part of the college experience.

By junior year I had a small circle of close friends who occupied most of my time. I started surrounding myself with more like-minded people instead of smiling like a ninny in everyone's face. These were the friends I prayed for all throughout my first two years of college. It's hard to pin point when we all met. But somehow I looked up at realized God answered my prayers. We became so close it was like we were all variations of each other. We had no boundaries, yet we never crossed the line with one another. When I wasn't at work I was somewhere in their dorm or we were chilling in mine. We held a healthy balance of companionship, love, respect, and patience within all of our relationships. These are the friends I'm going to tell my kids stories about while I'm putting them to bed.

Unknowingly, I fell completely off the grid junior year. I attended a few events on campus with my friends, but I was far less involved than ever before. I went to class, the cafe, work, and my room. I still smoked weed, and alcohol was no stranger to me, but I wasn't as social, I only talked to those in my small circle, minded my business, and went to class. I know how I said earlier I got serious about my academics, but I still needed to work harder after my perquisite courses. I studied speech communication and mass communication. I got a deeper understanding of people and human interaction. The different styles and forms we communicate verbally and nonverbally opens up a window for people to see who you really are. It was easier to "read" people, for a lack of better terms. I digested every lecture and every speech, hoping to fully understand the world of communication. Without communication, we are nothing. It's always intrigued me the way people thought and the way they behaved, hence why I chose it as my major and minor.

My perspective on people changed the way I behaved and the way I thought. Innately, I become a more reserved person. I'd become far more mature than the boy I was freshman year, desperately trying to make people laugh and form hollow relationships. Life became more transparent, and I grew into a person I had no clue lied within me.

In the second semester of my Junior year, I was high more than anything. I always smoked after class with some classmates. I wasn't buying my own weed, yet, but if some of my friends mentioned sparking up a blunt, I didn't refuse. Even though I was turning into a pothead, I started really excelling academically. Well, sort of.

My best paper was written after a long drunken night in New Orleans. The topic for the five-page paper was, "Is Martin Luther King still relevant in today's society and why?" I wrote it only hours before class. Had my professor known I'd written the entire paper after a night on Bourbon St. during Mardi Gras, I probably would've gotten an A on it, and had I not overslept for class when it was due, I wouldn't have had to turned it in late. She wouldn't take the late paper but I insisted, not even caring if she graded it or not. A week later she passed the papers back. She waited to hand me my assignment last. She placed it on my desk and told me to read my paper aloud. Looking down, to my surprise, not only had she given me a grade for the later paper, but it also had "Best paper in class, " circled in red right next to the "C" and big bold letters that read "LATE" across the top of the paper.

The closer I got to graduation, the more demanding my coursework became. My core classes were nothing like the prerequisite courses: more homework, more studying, more reading, more papers, and no more professors accepting late assignments. There were many moments throughout the semester when I become overwhelmed with all of my coursework. I had always wanted to be the best in the class. I wanted to write the best papers and give the best speeches. I was stressing out, and smoking seemed to clear my mind.

By the end of of my junior year, I was starting to make Dean's list, and things seemed to be looking up going into my senior year. Everything was starting to unfold before my eyes. Life was happening, I was maturing and learning about so much that I wouldn't have learned had I stayed home and skipped out on college. Going back home during breaks showed me that I was changing, inside and out. I dressed differently, and my conversations with old friends quickly grew stale. Even my grandma was getting on me for correcting her grammar all the time. I could see and feel things differently back home, and I knew I needed to continue the path I was on. It seemed like time was standing still while I was away from school during breaks. Each time I came back home, everybody was doing the exact same thing they were doing when I last left. Nonetheless, the year I thought would never come was around the corner, Senior Year. I was so close to becoming the first of generations to graduate from a four-year college, and my next move would be the most crucial.

CHAPTER 2

Decisions

I waited so long for my senior year of college to come, but once it came I realized it would be the last year of everything I loved about college; my friends, my professors, the freedom and especially homecoming. Homecoming was always my favorite time because it was the only period during the semester when I allowed myself to completely let loose and drink until I didn't know my last name. Along with the rest of college students everywhere, I was broke and my friends were broke too, and we somehow managed to keep each other afloat whenever we needed each other. Especially during homecoming. No matter how broke we were, we all had new outfits for the homecoming game and the after parties. In hindsight, I'm not sure why we put so much effort into finding an outfit because we hardly ever remembered the night anyways. The most I can remember is I had a cup in my hand wherever we went. I built an amazing tolerance for alcohol in undergrad. Back home during breaks at family events I would drink my older uncles and cousins under the table. They were impressed at how many shots of moonshine I could throw back without falling over thirty minutes later. Drinking everyday during homecoming week made me the new drunk my family got to know.

The first three years of college has to be the most carefree time of anybody's life, as well as the most crucial. College is recognized as the place to learn competitive skills for jobs in perspective career fields. However, in the midst of learning, we party, we drink, we smoke, we travel and live like there's no tomorrow. While, subconsciously, we balance our studies and learn how to live on our own. I eventually found that balance, but somehow I lost sight of the end goal. Somehow I was naive enough to think that everything would magically work itself out at the end of college, and that my dream job would just be waiting for me.

I thought getting through college was the hard part, and once I graduated I thought everything else would come easily. I went to class, I partied and made good grades, but I never thought about what was after college. Luckily, my professors and advisors were able to make me face reality.

When senior year started, I immediately concerned myself with trying to pump the breaks on what I knew was coming all along—graduation. Every year, I moaned and groaned about how I was ready to graduate and finally break free of college. I daydreamed about the day my family would come and see me walk across the stage. I couldn't wait to put on my graduation cap and take my graduation pictures. My mind was stuck on graduation and nothing else. But something clicked. I stopped living in the clouds and started to grind for a better future. I was so caught up in college life that one day I had an epiphany, which felt more like reality literally slapped me in the face and started snapping in my face telling me to wake up! I was walking down the plaza and it just hit me! I hadn't applied to any grad schools nor had I applied to any jobs. My passion for communication, public speaking, and television was growing the more I learned about the field. My professors were well versed in the communications field, I had no clue they were connected with people who worked in corporate America and the entertainment industry.

In one of my final courses, each student was set up with an internship that coordinated with their career aspirations. At this time, I was caught up in the hype with the television show "Scandal." I was hooked on the show, not because of the racy drama and the countless sex scenes, but because of how Olivia Pope got the job done. Her work ethic was unbelievable, her persistence opened doors, and her professionalism captivated me. I'm full aware that Kerry Washington is an actress portraying Olivia Pope—that she is just a fictional character in a make believe version of our world. But I knew that someone thought this woman up. There was an idea of a woman who harnessed so much power mainly because of her personality and wits. I wanted to be the male equivalent of Olivia Pope; a spokesperson, a reliable source of forward thinking, and a hallmark of adaptation. Therefore, I followed suit and I interned with the University's Office of Communication, working directly under the spokeswoman of JSU. It all seemed too real to be exposed to that level of professionalism and opportunity at the peak of my senior year. Full of purpose, I sought out to become that very person I saw in Olivia Pope. I knew I needed to get my foot in the door at a news station or start at a lower level communications position in corporate America. In my mind, it was only a matter of getting started. I was confident my work ethic would eventually take me to the places I vividly dream about.

My entire last year of undergrad was centered on this internship. Every morning I walked in to the administration tower, ready to learn and experience something new. I had access to the inner-workings of the school; all official publications, media coverage, interviews with prominent figures, and event planning all developed in our office. I took initiative and improved my skills by hosting and covering political events and writing articles on buzzing news going on throughout the campus, and near the end of the internship I co-led an interview that landed my name and my work in the one of the largest circulated newspapers in Mississippi, *The Clarion Ledger*. Although I thought that was the height of my collegiate success, I was wrong. My interview was read and discussed on a national level. My independent-study professor landed a role on Fox's newest series, at the time, "Shots Fired." Starring Sanna Lathan. Somehow I had to fight for my professor to get the spotlight he rightfully deserved. I thought this was a big deal, so I took his story to department's head editor. In a matter of days I was sitting across from my professor, recording my first real interview that would reach a national audience. I wanted to leave an imprint on Jackson State and I was doing so wether I intended on it or not.. I was made to talk, to communicate, and to create a common understanding between people through communication. For so long, I wanted people to hear and see my name being associated with meaningful and positive things.

I wondered though: was this the start or was it the end? I was accomplishing so much in college, but what was to come once I received my degree? I still didn't know, and not knowing was killing me. It helped that a lot of my classmates were feeling the same way I was, but when finals came around the corner, I was still far more stressed than I ever had been in my life. A few of my classmates were waiting on job offers, and others were going home for the summer to wait to start grad school in the fall. I wanted to go to grad school. At the very least, I would have liked to go home to have a chance to think carefully and plan out my next steps in life. But, this wasn't an option for me.

Everyone I knew was beyond proud of me for making it through college. I wanted my graduation picture to break the Internet. Of course, this didn't actually happen, but everyone on social media was so proud of me. All of my family and friends congratulated me endlessly on my new achievement. But, no matter how many likes those pictures got, no matter how many friends and family commented on how proud they were, it didn't make me feel better. I wasn't proud of myself. Instagram and Facebook made it seem like my life was going so great, but I knew the truth.

I had been away from home for four years, I was on the brink of entering the real world, and I still was relying on my mom for somewhere to live and would eventually be back in her pockets, begging for money. All this freedom and time away from home and I still hadn't built the self-sustaining life I imagined I'd be living by now. Four years before, I thought I'd be packing up my clothes and moving into my own apartment in a new city, starting my dream job, where I had to wear a tie and nice socks to work everyday. Instead, I was scraping up ideas in my head for what to do with my life. I honestly had no clue where to go once it was time to move out of the dorms. At that point, there was only one idea that made sense. I weighed the options over and over, back and forth in my head, and there was only one solution I could think of.

Join the army. Enlist. I told myself that all my problems would go away if I joined. Graduation was coming up fast and I honestly didn't have any other choice.

Life was sweet for my twin brother. He had been to Spain, Amsterdam, and lived in Germany all thanks to the army. He was living debt-free, worry-free, and even though I was always happy for him, a part of me was jealous. Life had been kind to him and it was starting to fall apart for me. The stability I thought I could rely on back home was crumbling, and I needed a safety net. My mom was dealing with a lot, this was a critical time I needed to rely on her, and she couldn't help me this time. My professors and friends kept pressuring me to apply to grad school and jobs, but no one knew what I was dealing with. My time was running out and I needed to find the fastest escape route away from everything.

While I thought that joining the military was the best option for me, I wanted to confirm that I wouldn't be making a huge mistake. Hasty decisions sometimes turn out to be the messiest decisions and I didn't want to make a mess up my life. My brother would be the only person I one hundred percent trusted to help me make a decision like this. This couldn't have happened at a worse time, but a man has to do the unthinkable when things get unpredictable, and I couldn't have predicted this in a million years.

At first, I thought I could just join the Reserves, which wouldn't have been so bad. The commitment wasn't as harsh as going to active duty and I could retain some of my freedom. But the reserves only offered half the benefits of the military, which wouldn't have been enough to get me out of the predicament I was in. I was left with no choice but to join Active Duty.

Talking to my brother every day brought us a lot closer. He knew I didn't actually want to join the army, and at first he didn't believe me when I told him. I had to explain to him what was causing me to go. He knew everything I wanted to do after college, and he told me joining the army was unthinkable. He gave me honest advice about his experience with the army, which was all news to me. Talking to him, I realized actually knew nothing about the army before I reached out to him. We talked so much just so I could try to get a full understanding as to what I was getting myself into. As the semester came to a close, I was quickly running out of time. Life was pressuring me to make a decision fast.

Once I made the decision in my head to join, that was it. I knew telling my family should've been the next thing on my mind, but it wasn't. I knew no one would believe, and if they did, they would've tried talking me out of it. So I went months without telling a soul, other than my best friend Bria and my brother.

The idea of it all, telling my professors that I wasn't pursuing another degree and telling my friends and family that I was joining the army, intimidated me. For certain I knew jumping into Active Duty right after college wasn't the ideal or nearly an expected thing for me to do. Especially knowing my personality my track record of throughout grade school. I was smart, but I stayed on suspension and always butted heads with my mom. It was clear early on that I didn't get along with strict authoritative figures in my life.

The decision to join the army would've never crossed my mind had I prepared myself to exit college and had my mom not told me what she told me. To be honest, I never liked the idea of being in the army. I heard the stories of PTSD, and the thought of constantly being told what to do made me want no part of it. Growing up, I made it known that if there was ever a draft, I would choose jail over war, and that was no joke.

In my mind, the decision to join was clear and understandable considering the circumstances. I tried hard to convince myself this was all my fault but, I shared the blame with my my mom. Her circumstances were my circumstances. My mom was evicted from her apartment back in Memphis. College was over and I was back under her wing, typically for most college graduates. However, to my surprise, by text, my mom told me she'd been evicted from the apartment she just moved into a few years prior and lost most of her things. Childhood memorabilia kept from our old house was thrown out on the street, and the new place I just started to call home was no longer my home. The text scared me. My mom hadn't said anything before about how she was struggling with bills or she was low on money. As far as I knew, she was making ends meet. At this point, I wasn't asking for fifty dollars every week. So, I knew it wasn't my fault why this was happening. But confused as to how and why this happened, and why was in the dark for so long? I didn't want to dig deeper than I needed to. Especially considering this wasn't the first time my mom had issues with our living arrangements..

Prior to college, my mom gave up on our childhood home. To this day, my brother and I never understood what happened with our mom and our house. Maybe the bills were too much, or maybe she was experiencing a midlife crisis. Whatever it was it caused us to abruptly move from the house in which we grew up. Senior year of high school was a rough time for my family. We were uprooted from our home in the middle of graduating high school. The entire situation put a damper on our accomplishments, but we never said that around our mom. We didn't know what was really happening and it was never like us to be insensitive to whatever our mom was dealing with. In the end, we sold literally everything in our house and still received no information about where we were going or what was going to happen to us. My brother and I thought finally we got a new bigger and better house. The sad reality was just the opposite—there was no new house at all.

We moved in with a close relative until my mom got back on her feet and eventually moved into a two-bedroom apartment of her own. During the holiday and summer breaks, I came home and slept in the second bedroom. My mom joked around saying she was finally free of her kids and had an apartment to herself. Fast forward to another senior year, another time where I was on the cusp of achieving something great, and all of sudden I get a text saying she'd been evicted.

My mom eventually called that afternoon, letting me know she was ok and was going to live with her sister. My aunt and uncle's house is a nice size and the invitation was surely extended for me to come and join my mom after college, but I couldn't. I couldn't impose on an already full house. My time in Memphis during school breaks weren't the best. I couldn't continue the trend of struggling during college after college. Had I returned home, I would have lost hope for a better future. I had no car, no job, and nothing in my life was sustainable enough to keep me on my own two feet. I couldn't rely on my mom, so it was time to rely on myself. College was hard, yet paying for college was even harder. Even when I worked two jobs, I was never able to save any money.

Had the news come at a different time it would've had a much smaller effect on my future. But, as it came just as I was about to graduate, it threw me off on planning for my future. Thoughts of, "what to do next with my degree" and wondering how to kick off my career quickly turned into thoughts of "where was I going to live?"

It's hard accepting blame for not being more prepared for life after undergrad, but it's even harder trying not to put blame on my mother for causing this dilemma. I still don't know why she didn't warn me she was facing an eviction. There was nothing I could do to help her, but she wasn't the only one who was being affected by the situation. She never gave me an explanation as to what happened and why she lost her apartment. I was left with a looming text message reminding me I had no place to call home. Why was I left out from what was going on? I was twenty-one years old, far older from the child I once was. I knew some things weren't my business, but I felt this was absolutely was. Had I chosen to pursue another degree, I still would've needed a place to go until the next semester started. If a job took interest in my skills, I still would've needed a place to call home. My life was in jeopardy just as much as my mom's was. Unfortunately, my hand was forced to do something I never imagined I would've had to do.

After all the FaceTime calls and all the non-stop talks my brother could handle, I finally concluded; no pain, no gain. "In order to be something, you've gotta go through something." And for sure I wanted to be something. I refused to let a circumstantial situation defeat me. The decision was already made in my mind, so the only thing left to do was to make it official.

I made the call to a recruitment center in Memphis and told them that I was interested in joining active duty. I sat on the couch in my dorm, knowing that this decision would change my life forever. My voice was shaky the entire call. I wanted to hang up after every question the recruiter asked me. I was so nervous, not because I was joining the army, but because I was afraid this would be a mistake, and I knew there was no turning back once I signed the contract.

I convinced myself that joining the army was an opportunity, not an escape. But an escape is what it really felt like, the easiest escape I could find. They were basically handing me my future on a silver plater, in exchange for my life, if I was called to war. But no other job offered what the army offers; room and board and a paycheck. It was all I needed, wrapped up in a four-year contract. I kept the entire process a secret until I signed the dotted line.

CHAPTER 3
Senior Banquet

Never in a million years had I dreamt this. I had always had wild ambitions, but never like this. I didn't want this for myself. What did I know about active duty, other than the stories my brother told me? What was I going to gain from having no control over my own life? If Uncle Sam said jump, I was going to have to say, "how high?"

As liberal and free-minded as I wanted to be, I had no choice but to conform to a world that rewarded complete obedience with rank and power. Disobedience in the army resulted in dishonorable discharges and possible jail time. Their laws and regulations were much different than the regular society in which I was raised. My track record showed no sign of favoring authority or any regard for rules.

Truly assessing the decision, it seemed like I was setting myself up for failure. But I told myself that thinking like that would only get in the way of my success. The army has it perks no doubt, the only problem was me. I needed to suck it up.

In a matter of days I matured into an adult by setting aside my pride in order to achieve a greater purpose. Somehow, I realized this was bigger than just me, I got a glimpse that my life's journey was bigger than I could fathom. For so long, my family struggled with education and some continue to be burden by finances today. Putting me through college was a struggle my mom couldn't handle. I struggled semester after semester hoping and praying I could afford tuition. I was sick and tired of struggling By first getting my degree and then joining the military, I sought to end another cycle of struggle, which my family has faced for many generations. No other job in America offered what the army brought to the table in exchange for zero experience. This was the way out. Serve my four years, reap the benefits, and pick up my life where I left it.

After the first phone call, I was set up with a personal recruiter. I worked diligently with my recruiter to make sure I left as soon as possible after graduation. All the while, I could feel the tension pulling at me, saying this was a bad choice. Trump had been recently elected, and the growing concerns about a war with Russia, China, and Korea intimidated me. I knew my family would try to stop me from going through with joining. We shared the same sentiments, and I knew that if they repeated the things that I was already thinking, I surely would have been deterred from joining. I didn't need reassurance. I was all the reassurance I needed. I saw things differently than they would see them. I was looking at the long term, rather than the immediate implications of joining. Despite how they felt or what they thought, eventually, I knew I would have to tell my mom and family what I decided to do.

The senior banquet was far more important to me then the actual graduation. My friends that had already graduated told me the entire graduation ceremony was quite boring unless you had a commencement speaker like Michelle Obama. But, I graduated a year too late to end up with her, and I honestly forgot who spoke.

It was only a long ceremony of listening to university administrators drawl on about "this giant leap into the real world." Instead, I opted to have my family drive down for my senior banquet to make the special announcement. The setting was more intimate and I knew this would be a huge surprise to my family, professors, and classmates.

Being that I was in the middle of finals, and I was in Jackson and my recruiter was in Memphis, we kept in contact through FaceTime calls and email. She was always there to answer all my questions. She told me I asked a lot of questions, but said that was good because most recruits don't ask questions. We handled everything from taking the ASVAB and narrowing down a military occupation without ever meeting in person. She made it known that eventually we would have to meet in person to sign some documents, to confirm my basic training post and job assignment. Since I was wrapped up with school, she eventually came to me. Coincidently, she was driving from New Orleans back to Memphis the same day as my senior banquet. Jackson was on the way back, and it seemed like the perfect chance for me to finalize my enlistment right before my family arrived. I could barely sleep the night before, and I ended up sleeping into the early afternoon. I woke up with excitement and determination in my heart. I was excited that I was starting a new chapter in my life, and I was fixed on seeing this as a positive experience, no matter what my family or anybody said after I made my announcement.

I cleaned my dorm and started to iron my clothes for the evening. In the middle of ironing, my recruiter called to let me know that she was thirty minutes away, and for me to send her my exact location. Shortly she arrived, and in no time we talked about possibilities of making a career out of being in the army. As we talked, we confirmed my military occupation/specialty (MOS) and the base I would be shipped to for basic training. The date was set for May thirtieth, a month following graduation. The only thing left to do was to let the cat out the bag.

Later on, my family arrived, and before they could even get out of the car they were pressuring for me to tell them my announcement. Of course, I didn't give in because they might have gotten back in their cars and headed back to Memphis.

It was hard to sit still through the ceremony during the banquet because, I was ready for the portion where the seniors got the chance to get up and speak. First we had to eat and sit through the endless photo slideshow compiled of events within our department.

But eventually, it was time. I was surprised to find that I wasn't nervous at all. I was more excited if anything. I tried to play off my excitement and eagerness by allowing a couple of my other classmates to speak ahead me. But I couldn't focus on what they were saying cause I was too busy focusing on my own speech. I had a table reserved for my entire family, and they sat front and center. I remember writing a few words down just in case, but I never ended up needing them.

I greeted the audience, thanked my professors and advisors for a life changing experience and education, and addressed the question: what's next?

"This decision was a hard one to make, and I've been keeping it a secret and I'm sure everyone is wondering what I have up my sleeve... well," I paused and glanced around the room and took a breath, "as of probably 30-45 mins ago, I confirmed my enlistment into the United States Army and chose my MOS as a 25Q, a Multichannel Systems Operator-Maintainer. I leave for Basic Training May thirtieth, at Fort Campbell in South Carolina..."

Either I imagined hearing everyone gasp or everyone actually did. As I tried to finish my sentence, I glanced at the table and I saw my dad cheesing from ear to ear, my grandma crying and smiling, and then I saw my mom. She was just sitting there, like she had seen a ghost. And that's when she got up and walked out. She got up from the table in the middle of my speech and stormed out of the room. Honestly, I was shocked, but I ultimately I couldn't care that she left. So I kept talking. I knew someone wouldn't take the news well but, I would've never expected my own mother to storm out the room. Nevertheless I continued,

"I know this comes as a surprise and I'm not sure how everybody feels about this ...."

My dad stood up and shouted, "I'm proud of you son! That's my son!"

I continued on, "But this was a decision completely made on my own. I prayed long and hard about making this leap of faith, and all I have to say is that God is in control of my life, NOT Donald Trump."

And I left it at that.

As I walked to my seat everybody applauded, and it felt like a sigh of relief to finally tell everyone what I had kept hidden for so long. All of my family at the table got up to hug me and congratulate me. I think everybody at the table was crying. There were a lot of emotions in the air and it was hard to contain myself. If I remember right I kept it like a "G" and I didn't cry, but I couldn't help but direct my attention to the two empty seats at the table. My dad's mom went after my mom shortly after she fled the scene. I asked everyone what was wrong with her and everyone just shook their heads in confusion and disbelief. I decided to go after her.

I walked into the hallway to find my grandma waiting by the bathroom and my mom inside crying. I sat with my grandma and talked and she fully understood why I did what I did and said that it was just a lot for my mom to take in. We sat talking until my mom came out of the bathroom sniffling and teary-eyed.

Trying to show empathy, I asked her what was wrong, but deep down I didn't want to. She explained that she was upset at the fact that I didn't tell her before I made the decision to join. Why didn't I tell her, and why was I making a decision like this?

Selfish, I automatically thought to myself. *This is so selfish of her.* But of course I didn't let that come out of my mouth out of respect. But I couldn't help but resent her for taking away from my moment, instead of waiting to discuss everything after the banquet. I thought I had every right to get upset, but I was never a hot head.

I paused and looked and her and said, "What else was was I supposed I to do?"

She replied with, "Tamarcus, we can find you somewhere to stay."

I explained to her that I didn't want to sleep on someone's couch. "What about a job? What about a car? What money do I have? What else did you think I was going to do?"

I explained to her that I was surviving only because Bria stepped in and helped out in a tremendous way, there was no way I was going to continue struggling back home.

After pouring out my heart to her, she just shook her head and said, "I can't believe you're doing this."

My hands dropped, my shoulders slumped, and I looked at her in such disbelief that she could possibly say that after everything I just explained to her. I couldn't sympathize with her, and I refused to repeat the same things I had already said. With nothing more to add, I said "ok," and walked away back into the banquet.

Despite the high emotions and embarrassment of the night, it turned out to be a success. I received so much love and support from everyone. Not everyone agreed with my decision, but mostly everyone supported me, which was all I needed. Dr. Bodie, for instance. One of my classmates told me she was at her table crying when I was up giving my speech. Dr. Bodie was like a mother to everyone in the department, so sweet and caring. She explained to me she wasn't happy about me going off to the army. She rather I furthered my education. Regardless of her concerns and tears, she took me by the face, looked me in my eyes, and told me she believed in me no matter what and that she knew that whatever I put my mind to I would succeed at! And then I was the one in tears.

CHAPTER 4
May 2017

The tassels were turned, the gifts and money finally came to a stop, and I eventually ran out of graduation pictures to post on Instagram and Facebook. Time was winding down. Although I had no home of my own to go to, I managed to convince my dad on the night of the banquet to let me crash on his couch for a month while I waited to leave for the army. At the time, I hadn't yet understood the true luxury of living rent-free. I was so eager to leave for basic training. I couldn't stop googling and watching YouTube videos on army life and what to expect for basic training. I was ready to get out on my own and make my own living. My dad and his girlfriend made sure I felt like I was at home, but I felt like I was hardly even there.

In the meantime, I spent the first week of May sleeping and eating my dad and his girlfriend's food. I had never lived with my dad after he and my mom split up. I only vaguely remembered him living with us when I was younger. But, during this month, I really enjoyed waking up and seeing him on a daily basis. I couldn't remember the days when my parents were married, so this type of interaction with my dad was new to me. He was so laid back and chill—the complete opposite of my mom. My dad likes to talk just as much as I do, and we ended up having a lot of great conversations. I picked up on a lot of habits and traits I observed from my dad, giving me answers to as to why I act the way I do. My dad was extremely goofy, which already knew, but seeing it every day was totally different. He was somewhat present in my life after the divorce but it wasn't consistent. Now we had the chance to lounge around and talk about whatever when he was off work. This was something I didn't know I needed.

While I was on my dad's couch, I made a list of things I'd have by January, once I was done with all the training, and I used this list as motivation to get me through my hardships. By January I'd be done with AIT, hopefully I'd be assigned to a unit in Germany near my brother, I'd have enough money saved up for my first car, and I'd be getting the first ten thousand dollar payout of my signing bonus. I kept reminding myself of those three things over and over in my head because I knew it wasn't going to be an easy ten weeks.

Now matter how much I wanted to think that May was going to fly by, it didn't. Everyday felt like it was two days in one. Every hour drug by like a snail. Once the thirtieth started to creep up, I began to start working out and conditioning my body for basic training. I did my research on army fitness and the PT test and started getting nervous. I had always been an active person but, never athletic. I didn't know I had to run as well as perform a number of sit-ups and push-ups in a certain amount of time. It made me nervous, but not scared. I was determined to make it through, so I began running and working on my push-ups and sit-ups every day.

On my first day, I tried to run two miles and nearly passed out. I timed myself at a good twenty-four mins. I ran like a fat kid but I wasn't going to be defeated. I kept running everyday. Sometimes twice a day. My dad told me he was impressed by my dedication. He said he didn't think I was going to ever get off the couch because all I did was sleep for the first couple weeks. I realized early on that basic training was going to be a challenge for me physically and there was a possibility I wouldn't make it through. I had to tap into a new part of myself to bring out the determination that it took to get me through ten-weeks of combat training with no phone, no music, no weed, no drinking, no anything. I figured this would be an experience I wanted to remember, so I decided to take a journal and write about the entire experience.

CHAPTER 5
Oath Of Enlistment

"I, Tamarcus Lott, do solemnly swear (or affirm) that I will support and defend the Constitution of the United States against all enemies, foreign and domestic; that I will bear true faith and allegiance to the same; and that I will obey the orders of the President of the United States and the orders of the officers appointed over me, according to regulations and the Uniform Code of Military Justice. So help me God."

I didn't sleep at all the night before I was sworn in. There was entirely too much going on in my head for me to clam down and get some rest. I was so anxious for the next morning. Everyone that shipped out on May thirty-first slept in the same hotel as me the night before. We all were headed to different states and held different MOSs. We each had a roommate to share the hotel room. It so happened that my roommate was also going to Fort Jackson in South Carolina and we had the same MOS. I instantly thought this was going to be my life long army friend, my "battle buddy."

But I was totally wrong.

I stayed up all night thinking. I imagined the endless possibilities and opportunities the army could bring. I prayed a lot, thanking God for this opportunity, because that's what I deemed it to be. An opportunity.

Meeting the physical standards to enter the army was hard, at least for me it was. All my life I've been relatively small, skinny. I was only one pound over meeting the minimum weight limit to enlist. I prayed throughout the entire process, ensuring this was the right move and if it was, God would grant me the opportunity to meet all the requirements to join the army.

Not only was this a job, it was a bridge to success. This was my attempt to make something of my life.

CHAPTER 6
Basic Combat Training

"**H**i, mom/dad this is your son/daughter, and I've safely made it to basic training at Fort Campbell..."

The phone conversation with my mom lasted exactly one minute. By now, she'd come to terms with my abrupt decision to join the army. We spent the last week together before I was shipped off, and she saw me off at the airport before flying to SC. It was important I had her support. Who else was going to write me letters while I was on lockdown?

The one minute they gave us was just enough time to read off the printed script that was handed out as we were assigned to our platoons. We were forced to hang up the phone after exactly one minute. After that, the drill sergeants confiscated everyone's phones. This was our last contact with anyone outside of Fort Campbell. After our calls, the drill sergeants gave us a tour of the grounds, the battalion, and the company training area. It would be our home for the next ten weeks.

I'm not sure where to begin on my first impression of the army. From the moment I stepped off the plane, my entire life changed. Everything was so new to me, and my mind felt like it was moving at a million miles per hour. I tend to a lot and I think deeply, too deep sometimes, and probably overthink things if anything. Any time I am experiencing something for the first time, I try to fully understand what I'm going through, hoping to see things from all perspectives of the spectrum, not just my own. So instead of using my charming personality and wit to maneuver my way through this experience, I decided not to. I decided to sit back and just do as I was told. Nothing less, nothing more. Be quiet, and follow directions was my guiding force. All through school, I went against the grain, talked back to teachers, and never followed directions. I did things my own way, and for once I wanted to be that quiet kid in the classroom that no one noticed. I was always the center of attention back home, even at school. Finally, I could take a step back to see what it was like to be the other guy in the room, the one who never spoke up and the one no one noticed.

On day 1 of basic combat training I was extremely focused and determined to be one of the ones who made it out in the end. I couldn't give in and quit. This was the one and only option I had. Nothing could have stopped me from not making it out of training. A car, twenty-five thousand dollars, and hopefully Germany was all on the line.

And I was right. Basic training was the most Hellish experience I've ever been through. At first, the training was kicking my ass physically. The running every other day was driving me mad. Running is cool when I'm the one in charge of saying when to stop and keep going, but not one someone is constantly shouting in your ear. We ran for PT every morning, we ran to chow, we ran everywhere. I had never run close to that much at such a fast pace in my life.

I didn't complain; I didn't gripe. But I hated every moment of it. I did what I was told when they were looking, and when they weren't I slacked off. It became a skill. I hadn't been there for three weeks and I was ready to quit. I was ready to quit far before this, but by the third week quitting was the only thing I could think about. This wasn't because of the training or the PT, but because I was surrounded by immature kids. I didn't realize, during the summer, that basic training camps are flooded with seventeen and eighteen-year-olds fresh out of high school. Typically, this is the time when parents kick their absent-minded, ill-mannered, poorly behaved child off the couch and ship them off to the army. I had no clue this was a thing. I saw in living color Mommy and Daddy's spoiled little boys become "soldiers."

However, not everyone in the company was fresh out of high school. Some had just finished college like me, others were simply at a point in their lives where joining the military was their last option, also like myself. Our company held about almost four hundred recruits separated into four platoons. Our battalion trained males and females. We did everything with the females except sleep in the same barracks.

My platoon was the worst platoon of the entire company. No one could follow directions, no one would shut up, and we seemed to have all the out of shape kids who couldn't keep up in PT. Every day was made worse because of how poorly our platoon followed orders and how frequently they stepped out of line. Honestly, there was never a time we could talk. We were always being told to shut up. I never said a word because it was pointless. There was nothing to talk about. Moaning and groaning to one another about how they didn't want to be there was only making things worse. We ALL hated being there, but complaining didn't make the situation easier. I'm sure I asked myself, "Who the hell raised these damn kids?" at least twelve times a day.

I mean this in the most genuine way, but I didn't know people could be so stupid. Literally, every night of training, the guys would do something incredibly dumb just as the drill sergeants entered to do their nightly inspections. Weapons were misplaced or left behind, some were caught trying to talk to the females in the stairwells. Both were plausible causes to have all the males doing push-ups or cleaning until one or two in the morning. Maybe it was the cleaning duty never cleaning, anything, or it was that out of two hundred huts only six knew how to properly make a bed to standard. No one could follow directions or do anything right.

I thought we were all born with some sense of basic comprehension skills, basic communicative functions, and basic knowledge. But a lot of these kids clearly knew next to nothing, and everyday they seemed to blow me away. The few times I did talk to somebody and tried holding a conversation with them, it didn't get far. After a while, I turned to my journal to get my thoughts out.

June 6, 2017, 09:45

"I feel like I've been put on mute. I've been here a week and I've said little to nothing. I just observe everything around me. Other than responding to the drill sergeants, I don't really speak. So much has happened so fast. All in one day, I got my uniform, got my hair completely shaved off my head, along with my beard, got measured for my dress uniform, received my dog tags, the list goes on.

This is the first time I've ever felt alone. College was my first time away from home, but this is my first time being alone away from home. I don't want to make friends because I'm surrounded by high schoolers. I'm already ready to go home. I hate it here. I'm surrounded by idiots. I don't know who the hell raised these kids, but they don't know shit, and they don't listen for shit. I have so much to say, I want to write home but I think once I get the letters back I'll become too sad and want to quit. The drills aren't that hard, at least for me they're not. I just do what the drill sgts say. It's just dealing with these seventeen and eighteen year olds is what's going to kill me, and this damn heat!"

-T. Lott

Every morning I was awoken by a blaring bullhorn and a screaming drill sergeant. The commotion would last for a couple of minutes, and once they were done I lied back down, closed my eyes and prayed to God, "Lord thank you for this opportunity, please give me the strength and patience to endure this journey you've put me on. In Jesus' name I pray, amen."

I did this every morning. It was my way of calming myself and preparing myself for a day full of training and pure stupidity. Because ultimately that's what it was, stupid. The drill sergeants played endless mind games. I always saw through the mind games but a lot of my younger battle buddies couldn't. Chow time, whether it was breakfast, lunch, or dinner, there was utter chaos. These were the times we developed a lot of discipline. We all were forever hungry because of the strenuous regiment but you could never tell anyone wanted food. Everyday somebody got it wrong. From day one specific direction were loudly and thoroughly demonstrated. By the end of chow we probably was running back to the training area.

They made us start calling each other battle buddies, I guess for accountability or something. But I was taken back by how naive and impressionable these teenagers were. This was the most many of them ever experienced outside of high school and they acted like it. It seemed like it was impossible for everyone to stop talking to one another. A lot of free time was taken away simply because we couldn't shut the hell up.

They believed whatever came out of the drill sergeant's mouths, even when it was obvious it was BS. Something in me wanted to step up and be a leader, but leadership roles in basic training come with an unbelievable amount of attention, criticism, and scrutiny that I did not want. I felt bad when my battle buddies were pushed to the brink of tears over simple lessons they could've, should've learned at home. Basic training was a game. The objective was to play the game and to not get played. Everyday the drill sergeants toyed with my battle buddies emotions. For the majority, this was their first time being yelled at.

Inside I was fine, my thoughts were flowing like normal, but I tried to mute myself. I was always in my head-floating away to a place where I mattered. I felt robotic waking io flung the same routine. I felt small and worthless but our drill sergeants always said, "the army is one big team, there is no room for the individual."

There was no part of the day I looked forward to more than the time to go to bed. Any other time I was being watched or told what to do and punished for not doing it like they wanted me to do it.

I was sick and tired of everybody's shit by the fourth week and was sure I was going to quit.

The drill sergeants and my "battle buddies" were on the verge of getting cursed clean out everyday. I didn't know who was stupider, the drill sergeants or my battle buddies. Some of the stuff that came out of the drill sergeants' mouths were unbelievable. Some of the drill sergeants were as young as me, and they were in charge of young impressionable teenagers.

The system itself was counterproductive. Instead of producing soldiers bound by real army values, they were just molding teenagers into their own image, mentally broken and damaged. The lessons and advice the drill sergeants were trying to teach I had already received in a more refined and conducive way in college. I'd already found the man in me. I knew who I was, and I understood how life worked. I can't speak for the whole army because this was only training, but I thought everybody in there was stupid.

෴

By the end of July, the thought started to settle in my mind that I actually went to college, graduated, and had a whole degree. I wasn't another one of these idiots with a gun. The more I realized what I'd accomplished, the more I got upset. I started to resent my decision to join the army. I felt like I was peddling backward. I wasn't making any progress in my life. I spent four years to get a degree and wasted all my knowledge by joining the army. I felt stupid and confused. Then I remembered what caused me to be here in the first placed and I started crying. I wanted to take it all back and go back to college and have a second chance at things. I would have this thought often, and each time I would have to hold back tears. I'd swallow really hard and quickly blink the tears away because it felt like I was blaming my mother for me being there, and I didn't want to carry her burdens on my shoulders.

I tried to make sense of what I was learning throughout basic training, but it was worse than high school. I thought learning mx+b was pointless, but learning to assemble and reassemble a M16 was even more useless in my eyes. There was nothing I learned that I was going to take with me in my career field. I had no interest in learning land navigation, or how to properly execute a reconnaissance mission. Whenever one of my battle buddies showed interest in the training I got so annoyed because I hated so much that I didn't want to see anybody else enjoying it. Rather than learning how to be the best solider I could have been, I was learning more about who I was without realizing it. I tried to hold on to the refined young man college developed me into. Instead, I was becoming a new individual.

"Hey, Bria,

I'm is not dead. I f***ing hate it here. I'm beyond ready to go home! I've thought about quitting literally everyday I've been here. But I have to act like a grown up now. It's hard to act grown when I'm surrounded by seventeen and eighteen year old lil boys.

The physical stuff we do isn't that hard. It's just these dumb a** kids who can't keep their mouths shut and follow directions. Anyway, what's going on in the world? I don't want to talk about what's going on here. Tell me what's going on social media, the news, JSU, tell me about you, ANYTHING to get my mind off this bull*. And did Beyoncé have them damn kids yet??"

-Tamarcus Lott

Eventually, I was confident enough to write home to my best friend and my mom. I'd gotten way past the point of needing something to take my mind off of all the negativity that surrounded me. Nothing we did was pleasant—it all was so morbid and stupid. The drill sergeants got a kick and giggles out of smoking us to death in the hot South Carolina sun. It was unimaginably hard to stay positive. Plus, all of my battle buddies ripped and groaned from day one. I don't think Bria knew how desperate I was to hear about someone else's life as a way to escape my own. In every letter I wrote to my family and friends, I talked little about what was going on with me because I didn't want to think about anything related to the army.

For some reason there was always a long delay in getting mail. We believed the drill sergeants were just too lazy to pass it out. A lot of others, including myself, would send letters back to back to get a faster response because it took nearly two weeks to get a reply from one letter. In that time, we were lost as to what was going on with the outside world. The drill sergeants weren't allowed to talk about what went on in the civilian world. But, sometimes they did.

On Sundays, which were our rest days, we had the option to either attend religious services or to sleep in late. I always opted to sleep in late. Around noon, the drill sergeants would come by to have casual talks with their individual platoons.

On one particular Sunday, as we were forming up for chow, I overheard some of my battle buddies talking about how their drill sergeant said, "Donald Trump declared war on North Korea."

I stopped in my tracks, turned around, and asked, "What did he say?"

She repeated what I heard and I refused to believe it. But as soon as she told me the news, I could hear the rest of the company murmuring the same rumor. I could hear the whispers and could see the fear on everyone's faces. Around this time, we were nearing the end of our training and had pretty much learned everything about basic combat training. Everyone feared we would be deployed into a war right after AIT.

At first, I wasn't quite as nervous as everyone else, because I hadn't heard it from the horse's mouth. But the more everyone talked on and on about how it could be possible, saying how our new president was liable to do anything no matter how foolish.

Instead of worrying and scaring myself silly as everyone else did, I waited until after chow and asked the drill sergeant who was claimed to have broken the news. He shook his head and asked me where I got this information. I told him I couldn't remember the exact person, and said, "Whoever it was told everyone you said Donald Trump Declared war on North Korea."

Instead of answering me directly, he gathered the entire company together and sat us down and explained what he told his platoon.

Donald Trump hadn't declared war. He explained to us that he simply told his platoon that tensions were rising between the two leaders. Someone took his words, mixed them up, and took it as far as declaring a whole fake war. I'm not sure who started the rumor, but this experience really opened my eyes and my mind.

A twelve-mile ruck march and a whole week in the field were the last training events before completing basic training. The war scare was all that I could think about the entire time out in the field. I was becoming a soldier, rather I liked it or not. I had no say so if I was going to be deployed or not. I had no control as to where I was being sent after AIT. I belonged to the army, and it frightened me that I wasn't scared or even nervous about the thought of going to war. I'd become so detached from my emotions that I failed to realize how my life could be flipped upside down on the drop of dime. I was far too relaxed about having no control over what I could and could not do.

Training was so close to being over and our drill sergeants became far more personable and relaxed in our last days with them. They even promised us that life in the army got much better after training. Training sucked, there's no other way to put it. I understand it's designed to discipline and strengthen soldiers physically and mentally. Therefore I believed the drills sergeant when they said life outside of training was sweet. My brother told me I would hate basic but just wait until I got to my unit.

❧

The very last days before family day were the days I was most talkative the entire ten weeks. I was so happy that my mom, Bria, my dad, and my grandma were on their way to get me away from all these idiots. I could've cared less about graduation; I was just ready to get the hell away from Fort Jackson.

Another graduation under my belt, and this time I was able to bask in the moment. I knew I was going to cry as soon as I saw my family. Hell, I cried when my mom mailed my JSU graduation pictures. I was miserable the entire ten weeks and I couldn't wait to be around people that I knew cared about me.

Celebrating the completion of basic training was monumental for me. Without me even knowing, my upbringing prepared me tremendously for basic training. I learned so many lessons as a child that gave me the upper hand to deal with the constant screaming and being told what to do. Being more experienced and understanding how life worked allowed me to see things for what they were, versus how they were presented to us. College broaden my horizons and I had a clear perception of reality, and life outside the army. I was already working towards the life I wanted have. For everyone else this was just the first step. Through understanding interpersonal communication and non verbals, I was able to read through a lot of the mind games the drill sergeants played, making the entire experience easier on myself. I can't imagine going through basic training as a naïve teenager. There was only one person I could think of that deserved a huge thanks. The only problem was I didn't want to admit it at the time.

At a young age, I said I would never thank my mom for anything she taught me. I was very stubborn and credited only myself for being "open-minded" and eager to learn. I'm sure as a child, your mom also liked to repeat the infamous words, "You'll thank me for this one day." But I vowed to never thank her. This day, however, was different. I knew without a shadow of a doubt I wouldn't have made it through BCT without the lessons and character my mom instilled in me as a child. During the time I thought I knew more than my mom, she proved me wrong time and time again. She raised be to be the man I was and still am today, and I decided it was time to give her the thanks she deserved.

My family took me to a restaurant as soon as we got away from the training camp. I had never been more excited to eat real food in my entire life. Once my family and I got seated at our table, we placed our orders and waited for our food to arrive. As we waited, I took the spotlight off of me and gave my mom her due diligence. A huge thank you was due to the woman that gave me birth. Being so much alike, we've rarely seen eye to eye. But there was no way I could have missed this moment to let her know that it was her that got me through the hardest thing I had ever experienced.

There were so many days that the behavior and character of the other recruits floored me. I was convinced that their parents sent each one of them off to the army because they were sick of dealing with them. My mom made it her business that my brother and I understood how the world operated and how to roll with the punches. She always told us we could do whatever we put our mind to. I never thought I'd join the army, and there were times I wasn't sure if I could make it through, but once I put my mind to it I realized how right she was. She equipped us with an endless amount of knowledge and determination. She taught us to stay close to God, and for that I told her, "Thank you."

I was so emotional in the moment that it was difficult for me to speak. At the end of my speech, I gifted my mom with my first military portrait. I stood proud and stiff in front of the US flag, with a mean mug and bald face in my army uniform. I wanted her to hang it somewhere she could always see me and be reminded that it was her that made this accomplishment a reality. We all cried the entire time because, when it boils down to it, my family is a bunch of cry babies and we all were still in shock that *I* sat at the table in my dress uniform as a solider of the army.

On August 13, 2017 I arrived at Fort Gordon, Georgia, home of the Signal Corps. This is the division of the Department of the Army that creates and manages communications and information systems for the command and control of the combined armed forces.

25 Quebec, a multichannel systems operator maintainer. For the next sixteen weeks, I would learn my military occupational skills. I was excited to learn, but even more excited to finally be free of my drill sergeants.

Even though I didn't know what to expect from AIT, I looked at it as another mission I was set out to complete. This time, I was less worried about getting through this portion of training. This was basically school, with which I had never had a problem. I always brought home A's and B's and college was a choice that I voluntarily made. I love learning. So I was very eager to learn my job. That was until I actually *learned* my job.

The first day of class was an exciting day! It felt like every other first day of school.

The atmosphere at AIT was far more relaxed and "fun" than basic training. Instead of drill sergeants, platoon sergeants took charge of us when we weren't in class; I guess you could look at them as really strict baby sitters. BCT was an intentionally stressful environment while AIT was the exact opposite. Every morning, of course, started with PT, and classes followed until about three in the afternoon.

After our classes, we had constructive conversations led by our platoon sergeants, mainly focusing on the army's core values: loyalty, duty, respect, selfless service, honor, integrity, and personal courage. I deemed many of the group discussions pointless and ineffective. Even the suicide prevention classes were useless. It was basically a class that summed up, "don't kill yourself", plain and simple.

Confined to the base, our weekends were spent as we pleased. Upon "phasing up" by taking a test questioning your knowledge on topics taught through BCT. Phase IV meant you had limited access to the base and couldn't wear civilian clothes. As you phased up you were given more incentives, like the chance to wear civilian clothes after duty. By Phase VI you were allowed to go off the base on weekends. I never bothered with the test. I figured going off base was just a way to blow money, and I was more interested in saving up for a car. For some reason I believed my parents were going to surprise me with a car for high school or college graduation. I thought those one of those accomplishments warned a new car but cars cost money and my parents didn't enough to make that dime true.

Although I felt more freedom, I maintained the quiet and standoffish demeanor that I developed in BCT. Although it was easier to be to myself here, I still showed next to no personality.

Instead of sleeping in a room with forty other guys, I was down to only three roommates. My reservations about the army hadn't changed since leaving BCT. In the back of my mind, I still couldn't shake the feeling that I had made a mistake. Instead of progressing, I felt like I was heading in the wrong direction. Everyone around me was just now experiencing parts of life that I'd already mastered. Two months post undergrad and I wasn't feeling any type of growth. Still optimistic, I anxiously waited for everyone else to arrive to AIT and for the first day of class. Deep down I wanted absolutely nothing to do with the army but, this was my life for the next four years, so I dug deep to be positive.

There were sixteen other soldiers in my class, and all were straight out of BCT from all around the country. Again, all fresh out of high school, a few females but mostly males; I was the second oldest of everyone in my class. I didn't talk to anyone. I found myself only listening in on open discussions and eavesdropping on private conversations as they talked amongst themselves before the teacher entered the classroom. The classroom reminded me of a computer lab. Each side of the room had two rows of desks, with computers along the wall and an open isle in the center of the room. I took the seat closest to the Smart-board by the instructor's desk. Our instructor was Mrs. Jenson.

Mrs. Jenson, a recently retired sergeant, led the introductions and kicked off the first day with a simple question. "What is a 25 Quebec?"

You probably could've heard a pin drop from the dead silence that filled the room. We all shared the same MOS. Remember my roommate from the hotel? He sat directly behind me, and we mimicked the same clueless look on our faces along with the rest of the class. Nobody actually knew what our job detailed. A few soldiers raised their hands and guessed at what term meant. We all knew the job description but not the job duties. We had let our recruiters pick our jobs for us, and just decided to believe them when they told us they were a good fit. My main concern was that the job came with a twenty-five thousand dollar signing bonus that would pay out annually throughout my four-year contract and partial student loan repayment. I was far more concerned with the money than knowing what I'd actually be doing in my MOS. Hell, with that big of a bonus I figured it was an excellent job. My recruiter and I had a number of talks about my goals and potential career path, so I trusted her with helping me decide my MOS. Before the end of class, I realized I had made a mistake.

Mrs. Jenson took to the Smart Board and started to explain what a 25 Quebec does and what we would learn during AIT. Ultimately, she explained that we provide communication to the warfighters through managing radios and satellites. We would be responsible for maintaining the equipment to provide Internet, phone service, and information to those carrying out missions both domestic and abroad. She explained the major importance of 25 Quebecs in the army, and the more she explained the more my spirit was dampened. I quickly started asking questions, trying to understand every aspect of being a 25 Quebec. Nothing she explained sounded appealing to me. Actually, the more she explained the more I wanted to walk out of the room. As she talked, all I got was AT&T telephone pole man vibes.

Since preschool I've always been ambitious about my career goals. Never did I think I'd wear a hard hat and shimmy up and down telephone poles and press buttons on a radio. I'm sure she read the disappointment written all over my face. I asked question after question to try and make sense of what she was telling me. I tried to make the job appealing in any way I could, but all of her answers were appalling. Defeated, I asked if I could go back and somehow pick another job. The rest of the class found this particularly funny. Annoyed by their amusement, I kept my focus on Mrs. Jensen. She was also amused, but she insisted that this was only the first day and that I should give myself time to learn what was to be offered before I jumped to conclusions. The long fancy name for my job was just that a long fancy name. However, signal soldiers, are referred to as "comms soldiers." We provided the army with communications. Whether it be communicating via voice, video, or encrypted messages, there was no army with the Signal Corps. But, the job was dummy proof. There was no real work, nor effort to be made. Despite my apprehensions the rest of class carried on with lesson one of the curriculum. As the lesson went on, I got angrier and angrier.

Unlike at BCT, we were allowed to have our cellphones with us at all times. The only time we weren't allowed to be on them was during class. I couldn't get out of class fast enough before I called my mom. I needed to talk to someone about the dilemma I was faced with. I explained in depth what was going on. I was disappointed to hear her give me the exact same advice as Mrs. Jenson; "It's just the first day, give it time."

I didn't want to give it time. I had no interest in radios or satellites. This was a *telecommunications* job. I graduated with a concentration in *mass* and *speech* communication, which is completely different. I love to talk. I love words. I have a passion to be heard, and I long to be on television just for that reason. I voiced this very thing to my recruiter. I was so confused as to why she matched me with a technical support job with no ties to any type of media production. The army offered jobs in public affairs, media production, and combat video/journalism. Instead I was just pushing buttons. I felt like I was swallowing the biggest pill when it dawned on me that I just spent four years of my life and over fifty thousands dollars in loans to learn how to speak, communicate effectively, and how to adapt to corporate America for it all to just be wasted. I didn't want to play with radios or transmit waves and push buttons. The biggest decision I ever made just felt like a big slap in the face.

Unsatisfied with my mom's response, I called my grandmother, my dad's mom. She helped me make sense of the whole thing. She understood my concern but insisted I look at the situation differently. She wanted me to keep an open mind and to learn everything they had to offer. Like all things, I was here for a reason. My grandma is a firm believer that everything happens for a reason; that all our steps are predestined. By the end of our conversation, she convinced me that I was there for a reason and that there was a bigger picture that I was failing to see. That learning this MOS wouldn't hurt anything and could only help and brighten my horizons.

Her advice got me out of bed every morning, but I remained in the same rut as before. No emotions, not talking, and completely shut down. I battled with sadness everyday. I hated my job. I wanted no part in learning a new trade that I was certain I'd never use again in life. I hated it so much that there was no way I could focus enough to learn anything in class. Mrs. Jenson often got irritated with my disposition. She would ask me questions about subjects she just explained to the class. I wouldn't have the slightest clue as to what she'd just went over seconds before getting my attention. I didn't want to know. I was getting paid to learn, so you'd think that alone would motivate me to pay attention, but it wasn't. I prayed for better days.

One day in particular (a Monday, to be exact), after spending the whole weekend praying to God, I tried to re-evaluate and reassess my whole situation. I didn't want to hate my job. I desperately wanted to love it. I felt defeated and it didn't sit well with my spirit. Monday was the start of a new week, and I was determined this day would be different. I woke up with a smile and held my head up. This was the first time my classmates actually noticed me, other than the first day of class where I put myself on blast for begging for another job.

Usually I ate breakfast secluded and alone with my headphones lodged in my ears, either watching cartoons or listening to music. Today, I ate with my roommates, whom where also in my class. Roylo, Milton, and Myles. I got to know them, and I also opened up a little. We shared stories about basic training and our lives before the army, and most importantly we shared laughs. Talking to them put me in the best mood since seeing my family. After eating breakfast we filed into formation, as we did every morning, and waited for the busses to take us to class. This morning, I finally felt ready for class. I promised myself I would listen to Mrs. Jenson and try to learn something today.

I made an effort to be happy. I was sick of feeling the way I did.

Mrs. Jenson walked in and to her surprise I was back at the front of the class greeting her with a smile. While she taught, I attentively took notes and followed along with her every word. The lesson was on routers, and honestly I can't tell you what else. It was so boring. I couldn't find an ounce of interest in any of the material. I didn't want to be defeated so quickly and I fought with myself, trying to stay focused. I managed to get through to the lunch break. Afterwards, everything quickly came crashing down in flames.

Mrs. Jenson picked the lesson back up where we left off before we were dismissed for lunch. This time, I couldn't keep focus. I tried, but I couldn't stop from thinking about how irrelevant it all was to me. I had no plans to make a career out of the army. I was in for my initial four years and then I was off to grad school. Therefore, I knew I wasn't going to pursue a telecommunications job at the end of my four years, no matter the salary. Nothing in the job description of a 25 Quebec would be pertinent in guiding me into the career path I wanted in or outside the army. I felt myself going backwards. I thought being well versed in all things communications would give me an advantage in the civilian sector, but I couldn't accept doing a job I hated.

As I stared off into space, I felt my spirit falling right back into the same rut. I laid my head on the desk in front of me while Mrs. Jenson carried on with lesson, and I started to cry. Just as quickly as the tears left my eyes, Mrs. Jenson noticed I put my head down in the middle of her teaching. She voiced her disbelief at the disrespect I was displaying by "sleeping" in her class. Demanding I wake up and raise my head, one of my classmates nudged me telling me to wake up. I was far too embarrassed to lift my head up and reveal the tears falling down my face. So I sat there with my head still on the table. Appalled, Mrs. Jenson called the liaison (the principal) to come remove a sleeping student in the class. At this point, I knew for certain I was in deep trouble. But I couldn't have cared any less.

After convincing the liaison that I wasn't sleeping, I poured my heart out to her.

I held nothing back. I made it clear I hated the job and wanted a way out. What were my options of escaping this hellhole? According to her, my only option was to get through AIT and wait until I was assigned to a unit, then to reclassify to a more desirable MOS. Had I chosen to go down that route and reclassify, I would forfeit twenty-five thousand dollars. In my mind, that money was already spent. Provisions were made prior to use some of my first payout to buy a car. I was devastated.

Heartbroken. The army was always a moment move, never a career move. At the beginning, I was open to making a career out of the military, but that was good as dead.

The rest of AIT was just that: a heartbreak. I carried the burden every single day that my first job right after college was not only that I hated but also one that I couldn't quit. As a kid, I watched my mom come home everyday from a job she hated. When I was younger she worked two jobs she hated. My mom tried to go back to school in hopes of obtaining a degree, ultimately to land a better job. It never worked out that way. She continued, for years, working jobs that weren't fulfilling. She had kids and bills, and she took care of us and paid those bills, but there's far more to life than just being able to pay bills. I didn't join the army to *just* pay bills. I joined to live better than those that came before me, but instead I fell victim to another hated job. What was worse, I didn't have kids I loved bonding to an empty career, but only a signed contract.

The only time I enjoyed myself was in the barracks with my roommates. Had it not been for my roommates, I'm not sure how my time would've played out. I was so miserable, but they were the keys to my sanity. They were younger than me and became my little brothers I never had. Roylo was insanely hilarious and we shared a love for music. We put each other on to some great songs. Milton seemed like he actually cared. The days that seemed to be the toughest, I found him in my corner, listening and sympathizing with me. He stood up for me when the other classmates would talk about me behind my back. Of course I faced scrutiny because I was the "oddball" of the class and I talked only to a select few.

And Myles. Myles and I formed a bond like no other. We related on a much deeper level than Milton and Roylo. The way Myles grew up was virtually identical to my upbringing. We talked for hours at a time. Nobody understood me more than my roommates. I confided in them and let them see the real me. Having a safe place allowed me to take each day as it came. I never gave up. Eventually, the sixteen weeks of AIT crept by, and on November 29, 2017, I completed AIT. I finished at the very bottom of my class. With the lowest average, I managed to graduate by doing the absolute bare minimum.

CHAPTER 7
December 2017

Apart from learning a MOS, AIT is where all soldiers anticipate receiving the orders that assign them to their first duty station. Honestly, you don't have a choice where your first duty will be. During the intake process I filled out a form, rating the top five states and the five countries to which I wanted to be assigned. The army houses soldiers all across the world, but I knew for sure my top pick. Germany. It went at the top of my list for countries. My brother served in Germany and right before separating from the army he met a German girl. She gave birth to his first child and later became his wife. When my brother broke news he was expecting a son, he made it clear to me he was staying in Germany to raise his son with his mother. He wanted a cohesive family unit, something we didn't have growing up. Of course my mom and grandmas couldn't begin to accept the fact that my brother was living across the ocean, in a foreign speaking county.

Despite the odds, they settled down, and it would have been more than perfect to be stationed in Germany with my brother and his new family. It gave me a lot of hope knowing there was a possibility I could be stationed in the same country as my brother and his new family. I prayed hard for Germany. It was the silver lining in my failing attempt to join the army.

On December 11, 2017, I was to report to Alpha Company of the 40th Expeditionary Unit at Fort Huachuca, Arizona. Not only was it not Germany, it was in the United States. All five of my top picks were out of the country. I didn't allow myself to be completely bummed by the news. I was excited for the change of scenery. I'd never been to Arizona and I'd never heard of Fort Huachuca. I had to ask a sergeant how to pronounce the name.

Fort Huachuca is three hours outside of Phoenix and a short plane ride outside Los Angles. I was still holding on to that piece of advice that the army gets better after training, and I was determined to stay positive.

After graduation, I was given choice to take my accumulated leave days and go home before the Christmas break or to fly directly to my unit and wait for the holidays to go home. With no hesitation, and with my twenty-third birthday only days away, I took a ten-day leave from the army to celebrate the three graduations I just had along with my birthday. I also just wanted time to reset my mind before heading to to my first duty station in Arizona.

The day after graduating AIT, some friends that I had made in college drove from Atlanta to pick me up at Fort Gordon. This was my first time back in everyday civilian life in seven months. I found this to be a bit overwhelming. I started to feel what I imagined inmates felt like after being released from jail. It didn't make it any better that our first stop was the mall, which was packed with people. On top of that I still had on my uniform, boots and all.

Everyone stared at me. From the the time I set foot outside of the car, until the time I took my uniform off, eyes were glued on me as if I was some type of celebrity. Soon I knew what social anxiety felt like, and it didn't feel good. This was all unwanted attention and I regretted not changing into civilian's clothes. I felt a huge weight of responsibility whenever I wore my uniform, especially now in public. People treated me like some hero. I was now a representation of the world's strongest army, only one percent of Americans make the decision to join any branch of the military. So I stuck out like a sore thumb. The mall visit was my bright idea—I desperately need a real haircut.

Three of the ten days I spent in Atlanta was with friends I made during college, Jared and Jared. They took charge of the turn up for my birthday celebration. I wanted to celebrate the end of a gruesome training, but it was too bittersweet. I barely mentioned anything about the army to them. I shared one or two stories, but I wanted to keep my focus off all things army. I was deeply embarrassed that I'd just signed my life away to the army and was wasting a degree I should have been utilizing. I made sure our conversations steered clear of that touchy subject. I was starting to make a habit out of bottling up my emotions. My birthday was coming up on the sixth; I had no business waddling in my sorrows when there was liquor to drink!

My time at JSU made me into a complete functioning alcoholic. Yes, I was mentored by the best, and learned a lifetime of great lessons, but I also built an impressive tolerance for liquor. I decided to take it slow in Atlanta because I hadn't gotten drunk since graduating from college. BCT and AIT was a drug and alcohol free zone. My mouth watered for a shot of Patrón. It was tradition to buy myself a bottle of Patrón every year on my birthday. In keeping the tradition, I made sure I visited a class six on base before leaving Fort Gordon.

My friends had no problem hyping me up for my birthday. They used any excuse they could to go out and get drunk. Normally I would too, but after a shot or two, I started to feel vulnerable and emotional. I could tell it was the liquor settling in and bringing all those bottled up emotions to the forefront of my mind. Intuitively, I stopped drinking. I let my friends drag me out to the bars, but I nursed one drink the entire night. I wasn't trying to end the night an emotional wreck.

They both pressured me each night to get drunk but I knew better. Nevertheless, my birthday was still a success and I had fun with my friends.

Next was Memphis. Just as I was trying to avoid conversing with my friends about the army, I sought to do the same with my family. I was still trying to understand my reason for being in the army, because at this point I was sure I made the wrong decision.

I was afraid of being exposed as a failure. No one knew my plan was crumbling before my eyes. To everyone around me, I was winning. But in my mind, this nothing but a failed attempt to show that I'd become a man and now I felt like I was walking around with a giant dunce hat on my head. If I known the army would've been a gamble between my degree and this new job I was given, I would've slept on my aunts couch. I didn't need anybody else validating that for me, so I shut myself off the entire time in Memphis. Locked away in my hotel room, I fell into a deep depression.

I waded in a pool of self-doubt and fell into an abyss of self-pity. Lying in the bed of my hotel room, I realized the sad looming feeling I've had since basic training was depression. I had never been depressed before, and I knew the symptoms. I had always believed that depression was something one could shake. I had always been an all around positive guy and never thought that a sadness could be so powerful or deep that it would cause me to not eat, or lie in bed crying for days, but it did.

I felt like my dreams had been crushed. Here I was, stuck in this militant, authoritative lifestyle. The deal I made with myself over the summer, while I was on my dad's couch, was that I would bite the bullet and do something that I knew I would hate, but in exchange I knew that the benefits would outcome the bad in the end. I remember telling myself, "no pain, no gain." But what was I gaining other than a paycheck? I was grateful for my paycheck, but what about my own fulfillment? What about college? What was that even for? At this point it felt like I was abandoning my dreams for security and comfort.

A long time ago, I made up my mind and said that wasn't going to be me. Now I was a disposable soldier. Although, in the civilian world, it's considered a great honor to serve your country, I didn't feel worthy of this honor at all. I felt like I was maliciously milking the army. Before, I felt like I was capitalizing on the army, now it felt like extortion. I put up half the effort to pass AIT, and I didn't want to take that same attitude to Arizona.

Despite the opposition, I mustered a new sense of ambition and determination to not be defeated by my circumstances. Depression wasn't going to defeat me. I had a bachelor's degree and I learned and researched some ways I could rank up and become a commissioned officer. It required some intense training, but with this spike of new hope and new ideas, I knew I could do it. I figured how I was going to manage through the rest of my four year contract. I thought about the advice of my sergeants and Mrs Jenson from AIT, and made a new plan.

This was a hard realization to come to because my mind was clouded by so much. I felt like my future was really at stake here. Every move had to be strategically planned, just as the decision to join was.

Before flying to Arizona, I tried making my rounds to see my family, but I couldn't. I only saw my mom before taking off to Arizona.

CHAPTER 8
Sierra Vista

Fort Huachuca is at the very bottom of Arizona. Base was an hour outside of Tucson in the small army town of Sierra Vista. I flew into Tucson on December 11, 2018, with a new perspective on the army. Flying high in the clouds always gives me inspiration, and overall I was excited for the move to Arizona.

All incoming soldiers coming from training are assigned sponsors from their new receiving unit, basically someone to welcome you to base and show you around, like a welcoming committee. My sponsor prepared me for what to expect from Fort Huachuca. I knew our experiences would be different, so I took his advice lightly. I could tell from the few times we texted we were complete opposites. Obviously, he cared about being in the army, and I did not.

He picked me up from the airport in Tucson and we made the hour drive back to base. I sat peering out the passenger window, observing the scenery of my new home. It was dry and dismal. Flat land, little to no trees, buildings, or people. The closer we got to base the more I could see that we were surrounded by mountains. My mind quickly jumped with ideas of hiking and watching the sunset. I knew the weather would be warmer than my usual, so I hoped to use it to my advantage. I was really disappointed with the fact I had to drive an hour to civilization. Nothing was in Sierra Vista. But, in general, I was focusing more on the positives and what this new life had to offer.

My sponsor gave me a tour of base, checked me into my battalion, and handed over the key to my barracks room all within an hour of arriving to the post. It looked and felt like a ghost town, but he mentioned that most of everyone took leave and had flown home for the holidays. I opted to take my leave days early to celebrate my birthday, so I was fine with spending Christmas away from home. I wasn't in the headspace to be surrounded by family anyways.

My barracks room came furnished with an old wooden twin bed, dresser, tv stand, and a desk, all in the same kind of wood. I wasn't expecting anything spectacular or luxurious. I shared the rest of the space with a roommate. He also was gone on holiday leave. The barracks were set up like my senior dorm. Your room was a suite and you shared the common areas like the kitchen and bathroom. I didn't mind having a roommate. I was ready to meet him, hoping that we would become cool and he would help keep me from thinking about how much I hated the army.

In college, I didn't have the money to turn my room into a man cave like I wanted. This time I did. And I had a lot of it. The entire time I was in training I was collecting a paycheck every two weeks, and there wasn't much of an opportunity to spend it. So I saved it and paid off some small debts. Now, I decided to ball out.

I wanted to make my room feel like home, so I did just that. Smack dead in the middle of the room I put a fifty-five inch LED smart tv, in the background I strung some LED lights that came with different colors and flash settings, a plush black rug on the floor. I blew two thousand dollars in two days. I didn't feel guilty about blowing a large amount of money because I had more saved up, and the first payout of my bonus was soon to be deposited into my bank account. So there wasn't that guilt of being irresponsible with my money. Honestly, this was therapeutic. Shopping carefree put me in good spirits. Once everything was set up and running I felt like I set the mood and my room started to feel like home. I was pleased and spent the holidays binge watching shows I'd missed in training. Christmas and New Years came and went and I barely left the room.

On January 13, 2018, I bought my first car with my hard-earned money. This was no small feat. I'm sure I can speak for both sides of my family when I say that nobody purchased their first car brand new off the lot in their name at twenty-two years old.

Once all the contracts were signed and the keys were officially handed over, I called my paternal grandma to tell her the news. But oh how quickly could I forget that she was one of the many other family members I avoided when I was back home in Memphis. Too excited to contain myself, I called her anyway. I apologized and forcibly told her what I was dealing with mentally and my reservations about the army. She gave me words of encouragement, got on my head about not seeing here in Memphis, and then we moved on and celebrated my first car! She was proud of me and I couldn't have asked for more.

Life was much easier with wheels. I thanked God continuously for my car. After arriving to my unit, I took full advantage of all that the army had to offer. As promised by my sergeants in training, army life outside of training was better. Much better. I felt free and could finally breathe. There wasn't a drill sergeant or platoon sergeant over my shoulder, ordering my every move. I appreciated the new freedom and started to embrace the army way of life. I hadn't thought much about my job because I was busy in-processing onto the base. This was a weeklong process and didn't start until after everyone returned from holiday leave.

Once the holidays were a thing of the past and the post fully reopened for business, I got well acquainted with Fort Huachuca. Finally I wasn't grouped with the rest of my battle buddies, training was over. I didn't feel suffocated anymore and I was free to be an individual. Training felt like jail, and I was finally free. I could now chill and treat this like what it was, a job. I tried to stop caring so much and over thinking, to just accept things for what they were.

The unit I was assigned to was very welcoming. At the end of my in-processing I was scheduled a meet and greet, one-on-one, with my First Sergeant and my Company Commander. I was afraid of holding conversations with members of my command team so soon. I wanted to get more acquainted with the lifestyle before talking to my higher-ups. No matter how I felt, the meeting was inevitable, as it was company protocol.

This was an informal meet and greet. The Commander and 1SSG wanted to extend the open door policy personally to each soldier that became apart of the unit. Cpt. Taylor and 1SSG Goss were incredibly humble and down to earth. Their interaction with one another was like they had known each other since childhood. Their tones of voice were calm and comforting, unlike anything I experience in training. Once they called me into their office, our conversation took a rather surprising turn. The conversation started off with a warm welcome to Alpha Company of the 40th Expeditionary Unit. Both Cpt. Taylor and 1SSG Goss gave me a brief history about their personal and professional lives. The conversation was handed over to me, and before this moment I hadn't really went over in my head what I cared to discuss with them other than my name and where I was from. But I thought quickly and tailored the conversation to my advantage.

I addressed the commander and introduced myself and made certain I brought up my college experience. Intrigued, I continued to tell them my predicament of how what I studied in college didn't align with my current MOS or my career goals. I explained the miscommunication between my recruiter. I laid everything on the table for them to understand where I stood in regard to everything. They exchanged looks after my rant and both of them shook their heads in disbelief.

Traditionally, anyone enlisting in the army with a degree would go to Officer Candidate School (OCS) and become a commanding officer in the army. Being oblivious to the workings of the army, I didn't take advantage of this when being recruited. But now it was my second chance at a great opportunity, I just needed guidance. They both offered to help me out of this pickle, but it wouldn't come to fruition until much later.

I got word back in AIT from my sponsor that my unit was about to deploy to South Korea. I was nervous when I got word that I could have possibly been deployed. He wasn't sure if I was on the list to go, and I was told not to rule out the possibility. It wouldn't be until I arrived in Arizona to know if I was headed for Korea or not. However, when I arrived I found that it wasn't a deployment but a routine rotation between units. One unit spends six to nine months in rotation, and at the end of that, another unit replaces that one to continue providing services abroad. I was very nervous and skeptical about this mysterious list. It wasn't posted anywhere. The people going just knew they were going. I wasn't sure if I wanted to go to Korea or not. I honestly didn't know if I wanted to go off to another country or stay in Arizona. Both were new to me, but it wasn't for me to decide. Nonetheless, I was one of the few that stayed behind at Fort Huachuca, while the majority of our unit prepared for Korea.

In the short amount of time that passed from January to February, I made acquaintances with a number of the soldiers in my unit. My persona was much different from that during training. I was almost back to Tamarcus, not fully, but I was getting back into the swing of things. Still reserved but happier, I started to make a home in Sierra Vista.

CHAPTER 9

February

*I**t's amazing how you can fall asleep on top of the world but when you wake up it feels like the weight of the world is on top of you.*

    I forced myself proud of my decision to join the army, and was hopeful about the future as an active duty soldier. Life couldn't have been any more sweet, so you'd think.

    It all came to a screeching halt the day I officially reported to my sergeant for work. Now is a good time to mention how I was using every excuse in the book to put off reporting to work. I lied about in-processing, saying I had more to do when I didn't. I failed to report to PT formation for about a week. I tried to stay under the radar, so I could play hooky for as long as I could. I was dreading reporting to work. I didn't want to face that monster just yet. I tried desperately to buy myself more time to cope with the agonizing reality of working a job that I barely knew about and I knew would give me absolutely no fulfillment.

    It was high school all over again. The days when I just didn't feel like going to school, I would play sick or just blatantly skip the entire school day. Of course, I got caught and suffered the consequences, but I was prepared for any punishment my mom dished out. I cared enough to make sure my grades were good before I decided to skip school. This time, I didn't care about the consequences; I didn't care about failing to report to work. Hell, I was the new guy, so I figured nobody would really be looking for me, but one morning this was proved wrong.

    Awaken by vigorous banging at my door, I jumped up out of my sleep, startled by the noise. I was too afraid to answer the door. It was well after 0600, so PT was over at this point. I was certain my time ran out of playing hooky and and my cover had been blown. My heart was racing. I was scared at who it could've been. The banging continued, whoever it was was very adamant about waking me up. Stubbornly, I sat in my bed waiting for whomever it was to leave. Eventually, the knocking stopped. Relieved, I laid back down and attempted to go back to sleep. Just as soon as I closed my eyes, I could hear footsteps and chatter coming from behind me, right outside my window. Every night before bed I would crack my window to let a breeze in to keep me cool at night. Biggest mistake ever. As I tried to make out the noises coming from outside my window, someone tapped on the glass and called out my name, "Private Lott!"

I froze, praying they would go away if I didn't breathe or move. The taps turned into banging and I turned my head to try to peak outside my window to see who it was. As soon as tilted my head towards the window, a pair of eyes locked with mine. I turned around to see who was persistent enough to come to my window for me to get out of the bed. There stood three sergeants peering through the window at me. Each of their faces was marked with disbelief and anger. Quickly, the sergeant who called out my name told me to get dressed ASAP and report to the company office. This would be only the first of many mornings where a sergeant would have to come drag me out of bed.

I was let off with a warning this first time. It was easy to play dumb in the army because, to be honest, a lot of new soldiers aren't the brightest. A lot of recruits choose the army because they couldn't get into college or they were just plain and simple. Therefore, everything was broken down in the simplest form and explained to us as if we were children. I acted as if didn't know any better, and that was my way out of any trouble I faced during training. I was just another "dumb private" to them. Although it was sometimes hard for me to play this role because many of my officers knew I was a college graduate, so a lot of the cadre didn't believe I was as dumb as I acted. Now, I finally got caught slipping out on work. I had no choice but to show up to formation the next morning.

It was as if I were a celebrity guest at call formation. Everybody was staring and mumbling, "There's Lott. There's the new guy." I'm guessing my name was called every morning and everyone was wondering when I would finally show up. It should've been embarrassing, the entire company was wondering who the hell I was. The Company Commander sent a search party out for me and I was unfazed by the entire ordeal. I created a heap of unwanted attention for myself.

After PT, personal hygiene was conducted, and there was time to eat breakfast before 0900 work call formation at the motor pool. I'd never been to the motor pool, but I heard about it during AIT. Like many other army things, I didn't know what it actually was. But when I arrived and filed into formation, everyone got sight of a new face and quickly began to realize I was "Lott," the new soldier that they were looking for everyday. Just like that I went from the quiet guy to the center of attention and I hadn't even said a word. Formation went on as protocoled and the battalion commander dismissed us to our designated work areas.

"Motor Pool Monday." The motor pool is a large lot of all of the military vehicles assigned to the unit. Our unit was the only force command unit on base. Meaning if an immediate threat was to hit Fort Huachuca or the surrounding areas, our unit would be the first unit to respond. With that being said, all of our vehicles had to be ready for dispatch at all times in case such an event happened. Thus, this took up the majority of our job duties: maintaining vehicles. Monday through Wednesday was motor-pool maintenance, including checking oil and tire pressure, replacing filters, and fixing other problems that cars and trucks could have.

The first week I skated by doing the bare minimum. I didn't work on any trucks. I stayed out of sight and lallygagged around the motor pool. I watched others work and pretended like I was watching and learning; meanwhile, my mind was far from learning anything.

That only lasted for so long before I grew bored of twiddling with my thumbs and scrolling endlessly through social media on my phone. I couldn't believe my life. It felt like I was constantly peddling backwards instead forward. What the hell did I go to college for if I was just going to end up a mechanic in the army? I felt more and more like a waste day by day. In college I had a great sense of purpose, but what was my purpose in the army? Was my only purpose now as a solider is to take orders? I was sitting on four years of education, ready to apply it to my everyday life. But nothing in my everyday life required that level of philosophy or problem solving. I felt mediocre and useless. Most of what we learned in AIT was never addressed and I wasn't sure when I'd actually work the MOS I was given.

College made the army seem like a living hell. The idea of joining the *army* after college started sounding more stupid by the day. I was in the middle of a culture shock. It was hard adapting to the conservative, suffocating, dictating world of the army and there was no off button. This was now an everyday, all day thing. Even after five pm, after the workday was over, I was still at will to the army, on call 24/7. My life was always in the hands of someone else and I was constantly being told what to do. Four more years of feeling what I'd already been feeling was scary. My mind had never been so clouded with sadness. The emptiness I felt every morning when my alarm forced me out of bed for PT was depressing. Every day I anxiously awaited the end of the workday just to retreat to my barracks room where I could be alone with no one to bother me.

It became monotonous. The same routine every day was driving me crazy. Weeks began to fly by without notice. Everyday was exactly the same. Wake up, get dressed for PT, conduct PT, shower and eat breakfast, sit in my room til the last possible second, then report to work, break for lunch, and by the end of the day you could've found me somewhere staring off into space, not doing what I was told to do, waiting to be released for the end of the work day. Nothing changed unless random orders came down from our command team to carry out. Otherwise, I was living on autopilot. I couldn't help but feel like my life was wasting away. My everyday life was planned by somebody else, controlled by someone else, and watched over by someone else. My time was divided according to the needs of my unit. I didn't have to think for myself. The army did all the thinking for me. Mentally defeated, I drifted back into depression without knowing it.

My life lacked spontaneity. My life lacked meaning. My life was not my own. I anxiously waited for the weekend to rejuvenate and find a life of my own outside the confinements of Fort Huachuca. I was extra happy I had a car now and could make the drive to Tucson. Every weekend I made the hour stretch to the city in hopes of finding a friend, a restaurant with great food, or anything that would give me something to look forward to. The weekend was an escape from the uniform. The uniform came with great deal of responsibility and a heavy burden. The weekend was the perfect opportunity to get my mind off of the things that made me unhappy. I was set to make this work. Something had to give and it wasn't going to be me. I made the decision to join, so it was up to me to find happiness within this decision.

CHAPTER 10

Conformity

The military's target audience for recruitment is upcoming seniors and high school graduates looking for a chance to break free from their mom and dad's reigns. Recruiters do an amazing job of selling the army to its recruits. Free college, endless opportunities to travel the world, retirement options, and let's not forget your signing bonus, these were all things promised to me by my recruiter—which all were true, but she forgot to mention the price I'd have to pay in return. Because nothing is life is free. Virtually, it seemed as if this was a handout. It all seemed too good to be true, right? A brand new car, a twenty-five thousand dollar signing bonus, free healthcare across the board, a meal plan and a place to live. All of it seemed like it was just given to me.

At first, I saw this as the greatest opportunity to get me out of the predicament I was faced with as I was coming out of college. That was until I entered into the depressing world known as the greatest fighting force on the planet. The person I was in college compared to the person I was in the army were complete strangers to each other. Everyday I was drifting further from the person I once was. Don't get me wrong, serving your country, and risking your life for the safety of others is the ultimate selfless act. But the "discipline" they wanted to instill in me tried to rip me from everything for which I stood. Serving my country wasn't my driving force for joining, but I knew my job came with a great deal of respect and honor. But, again, at what cost?

America was built upon the idea and values of freedom and independence. But I felt like my freedom and independence were the very things I was being robbed of.

Being a soldier is not a job, it is a lifestyle. From how you make your bed in the morning to the way you shave your face at night, there's always a looming feeling of war. Everyday is preparation for war, disregard politics and tensions overseas; your job is only centered around two things: survival and war. Even in peacetime, the army is still preparing for war.

A lot of the "brainwashing" I heard about as a child began to make sense. Not only did I have loved ones who served in the military, I experienced first hand them returning home as a new person. Whether they had served in war zones or were never deployed, they always returned home in some way different. As kids, my cousins and I often steered away from our cousin and uncles returning from the military because we heard the crazy stories of PTSD. We didn't know for sure what it was, but we weren't sure if it was contagious or not, so we veered clear of those coming home from the military.

Full circle, I was now beginning to understand that "new person" I recalled seeing in my loved ones. It wasn't PTSD. It was the climate, the everyday life of the army. It's life changing. From the start, in my eyes, basic training resembled a failed attempt of fathers trying to turn boys into men. Quickly being thrown into an unknown world meant having to adapt quickly. This required a lot of sacrifice that I never foresaw. Nothing I learned prior to the army truly mattered. College seemed like a complete waste. I was no longer a student. I was a soldier training for combat. It was only what I learned during training that prepared me for the lifestyle of active duty. But I felt as if I was abandoning my previous life for a new life that I didn't even want.

From a distance, I paid attention to my battle buddies throughout training. From day one I watched them, captivated by how easy it was for the drill sergeants to strip away everything their moms and dads taught and dreamed up for them. Personalities changed, morals changed, perspectives changed, all over the course of ten weeks. Years of outdated rhetoric and false entitlement were stamped into the minds of my teenage battle buddies. This was not the case for everyone, but it was widespread enough to cause concern within my own mind. I watched the individuality be snatched blindly from a lot of my battle buddies and molded into what the drill sergeants saw fit.

    I refused to conform because I didn't want to be made into a new person. I liked the person I was already made into. The lessons my mom taught me were much more valuable than those the army tried to teach me. College developed my mind well beyond the strict rhetoric of my drill sergeants.. I was a man in every aspect of life beyond my finances. I walked, talked, and conducted myself like a man—my bank account just looked a little childish. My immature ways were long abandoned before I thought to join the army. I didn't accept the coercion forced on the weak minded. My mind was stronger than ever and needed stimulation to thrive. College adequately made me who I was, while the army tried to create a new me, suitable for war and a sacrificial lifestyle, sacrificing far worse than I ever imagined for myself. There were more ways than one to effectively build a soldier fit for battle. This particular system proved to work in previous war times but now it is outdated and harmful to the minds of our youth.

    Individualism is strongly rejected in the army. The very things I knew that distinguished me from others no longer proved relevant. Individuality threatened the idea of uniformity and obedience. I wanted to be different. I didn't want to fit in with the rest of the team. I knew I thought differently than my battle buddies; I was the black sheep of the herd. It was rather difficult accepting the culture and traditions of the army when I knew it was all a made up world. It was a man-made society. I was no longer measured by intellectual abilities, but by the capabilities of the work I could produce. I no longer wanted to be an addition to this made up society. I wanted to be an addition to a society that mattered. I fought tirelessly against the suppression of individualism. It was an inward battle. On the outside I was a blank canvas. Nobody really knew how much it bothered me to be a part of the greatest army in the world. I didn't want it to bother me. I wanted to like it. I wanted to like it desperately. I tried finding enjoyment in the smallest of things because at the end of the day I always want to succeed at everything I put my mind to. However I seriously never thought I'd ever join the army but here I was, going through the motions like a zombie. With no purpose, I drove myself to the darkest depths of…

CHAPTER 11
Depression

"Relax, it's easy money." I can't tell you how many times I heard this phrase.

I can think back to a phone calls with my dad when I was in AIT. He was one of the main ones saying, "It sounds like easy money to me." I get my strong sense of curiosity from my dad because he wanted to know every detail about my job. He wanted to learn as I learned. Instead of complaining to him about how I hated the job, I let him learn about my MOS as I did. Everyday I called him and told him what I learned. I even snuck and sent pictures of some of the equipment we were working and training on. It didn't take much for him to realize that this was something I had no interest in. He knew the job sucked, and his realization validated every emotion I was feeling throughout AIT.

Ultimately, I joined the army to build financial stability, which I. Money was no longer a hassle, I had a roof over my head, a brand new car, and a new fit for every day of the week. The only thing that was missing was my own happiness. I couldn't find happiness within because I was looking for it within my job. We were all put on this earth for a purpose. At one point I thought I knew my purpose, but now the army had me questioning everything. Nothing I did created a sense of purpose. Why was I here, other then to collect a check on the first and fifteenth? I didn't belong. I ostracized myself from the remainder of my unit. I hardly spoke. I needed answers on why I ended up here. There had to be more of reason for me to join other than not having a place to live. There was no foreseeable way to make the situation better, so I accepted the fact I was stuck unhappy for the next four years. I felt defeated by my circumstances. I caved in to the emotions clouding my mind and heart. I accepted the loss of an opportunity to better my future. I stopped caring about the army. I stopped caring about everything. I ended the efforts to find an alternative route to pursue a job fitting for my career path.

I drove to a bar every other night after work. I ordered the same ten-piece mild wings followed by rounds of drinks and shots. I drank alone until I got to the point where tears started to form in my eyes. I drank myself miserable every night after work. Drinking became part of my daily rut. I let the stress of life consume my mind so much I ended up crying myself to sleep many nights after leaving the bar. I'd cry myself to sleep hoping that I'd disappear by the morning and wouldn't have to face the agony of another day.

Drinking was no coping mechanism. I drank purposefully to be sad. I tried to figure out a way to be happy. The only thing that made sense was to cry out the sadness. I drank and cried in hope of a breakthrough. I was crying out, hoping if God would feel so sad for me he would somehow change all of this for the better. I couldn't see or think past what was going on at the time. I just went with the flow and got caught up in my current misery. I hoped for so much out of this relationship with the army. It was way too early to regret this decision but I didn't need four years to come to the realization that I was unhappy with my life.

Nobody saw the dark heavy cloud hovering over my head. I saw it. I felt it haunting my every move. I couldn't escape the daily darkness.

But, after a while I was willing to endure the darkness. I realized I was getting in my own way of success. Like my dad said, like my brother said, like so many others said, "It's easy money." I was not signed to the army for the rest of my life! It was only four years, four years of saving money. Because ultimately that's why I joined, for the money. Why was I letting my emotions control me? I felt like a punk, crying over spilt milk. All of sudden I got frustrated with myself. I refused to let my emotions dictate my future. I was drowning myself in sadness. I was finding every little thing to remind me of the degree I wasn't using.

Plainly, I got tired of being sad. Everyone in the company thought I was some psychopathic weirdo who never talked. Nothing I did, reminded me of my former self. All my life I had been an advocate for positivity and change.. I'm a firm believer of looking at the positive side of things versus the negatives. I'd never seen myself so down in the dumps about anything before, and I suddenly knew I had to overcome this sadness and prosper.

I took control of my emotions just like I took control of them during basic training. I hated everyday of basic training but I got through it. I didn't think about the negatives. I thought about everything except for what was going on at the present time. I was certain I could overcome it if I took my mind off the things that kept me unhappy. There were people in much worse situations than I was, so why was I letting this little hiccup bring me down so low?

I was far from happy, but I tried to push on. If the army had taught me anything at this point, they taught me how to endure the toughest of situations. I told myself no more crying, no more calling home to my family and complaining. I had to be a man and step up and own this decision. I wanted that so desperately. I wanted to shake loose all the bottled up emotions I was harboring. Which vividly reminds of AIT.

Myles, my roommate, bought some sleeping pills from the PX on base. I'd really never thought about sleeping pills before then, and I wasn't sure if they would work when he told me about them. But he took them one Saturday morning and slept the whole day away. Eventually sleeping beauty rose from the dead and his reaction was all that I needed to know. Myles was having trouble sleeping but I on the other hand just didn't want to be awake when I didn't have to be. He literally slept the entire day and that did it for me. I headed to the PX and bought three boxes. In AIT, most of our time not in class was leisure time. But I didn't want leisure time. I wanted a way out, and the only way I could find one was by sleeping. I popped a pill after class everyday. By the time we finished eating chow I was ready to sleep the evening away. There was no class on the weekends, so I took a pill twice Saturday and Sunday. I stopped taking the pills once I got to Arizona. I figured the change of scenery and the end of trading would boost my morale. It did for a day or two but I started back taking the sleeping pills and alternate between drinking after work.

Morning after morning I woke up later and later for PT. In my mind I wanted to get up. I knew it would cause trouble for me later, but I literally couldn't get out of bed some mornings. Needless to say, it started to become an issue. My platoon leaders took notice to my tardiness. No one knew I was taking pills to sleep or drinking myself to the point of tears.

Usually I was the very last soldier of my entire battalion to make it to the PT field. I'm sure everybody thought I was making the walk of shame by strolling up to formation minutes before saluting the flag. I didn't care about the smack my sergeants dished out for being late. I cared even less about the disrespect I showed my command team. All I cared about was that I made it there in time to salute the flag and conduct PT. Not longer after that, however, I stopped caring about everything. I eventually stopped setting my alarm for PT, which led to more sergeants banging on my door and blowing my phone up demanding me to get dressed and report to the PT field. And each tardy or absence resulted in disciplinary action.

Write up after write brought me closer to an Article 15; essentially a formal referral for disciplinary action. Depending on the level of offense, I was at jeopardy of losing my pay, being demoted, or charged with extra duty—the list goes on of possible punishments I could have faced. Still, I didn't care.

As a result of my blatant disregard for rules and authority, I was served my first Article 15. Five days of extra duty was my sentence. FTR or failure to report to PT formation and failure to report to work call formation were my offenses. Being that the offense was so low and correctable, my company commander gave me the lowest grade of an Article 15. A company grade Article 15 meant that it wouldn't go on my permeant record or deter me from any additional benefits, like going to certain schools where I could receive specific certifications within my job. Basically, it was a small probation period meant to reprimand my misbehavior.

I'd created a name for myself within my unit. I was the weird guy that barely talked and did no work. I was a present body during the workday but completely absent minded. Again, I skated by doing the absolute bare minimum. Like everybody said, "it's easy money." I made it even easier.

Something ate at the back of my mind every single day. I always felt bothered by something. I had an attitude for what seemed like no reason. It was like the devil himself was whispering in my ear trying to sabotage all my hard work of trying to make a better life for myself.

Have you ever looked into the eyes of someone who was present-body but absent minded? Because apparently everybody around me knew there was something wrong with me. I didn't talk much, nobody knew the *real* me, but yet, everyday somebody stopped to ask me, "What's wrong? You ok?"

I guess they could see through the facade I hid behind. I never admitted to anyone how I was feeling. I carried that weight alone. I didn't want to become a "special case" like my bunkmate from boot camp. He was put on suicide watch after confessing he was depressed and home sick. I didn't need others feeling sorry for me, so I kept it to myself. I always looked confused when they asked if I was ok. I would snap out of it for a second just to reply, "Yea, I'm ok."

I wanted to to shake this feeling so badly. I wanted to like the army, and I desperately wanted to love my job. I needed this opportunity more than ever to set me apart from the competition in the real world. I knew deep down that being there was a good thing for me in the long run, so why couldn't I just get with the program and finish out my four years? Instead, I was a lost soul praying for a silver lining.

CHAPTER 12
90 Days

A typical workday in the army ends around 1700 or 5:00 PM. My extra duty for the Article 15 started promptly at 1800. That was only enough time to drive off base to grab a bite to eat and drive back to report for my extra duty assignment. I was told an extra day would be added for every minute I was late for extra duty. This had to be the longest five days of my life. On top of dreading the normal workday, I had to suffer through four more hours of it.

I stripped and waxed floors, raked leaves in the cold, and cleaned bathrooms and toilets. Each day I thought about not showing up for the extra duty. I even contemplated going a-wall. But, deep down, I knew I was just over-reacting to a small punishment. It wasn't that bad, but I defiantly didn't enjoy any of it. I worked every night until 10:00 PM, while everyone else ordered pizza and played video games in the barracks. By the time I got to my room I was too tired to do anything but undress, shower, and go to sleep.

During this time, I tried to get my act together. I tried to be the perfect soldier, but this life was just too comfortable for me. Everything was being handed to us. I kept psyching myself out, telling myself this was something that it wasn't. At one point the army was intended for dummies who couldn't get into college and couldn't crash in their parents couch anymore. That might not be as true today but, the army still operates in that way. Even one of the drill sergeants said, "you're all here because you were to dumb to get into college or your parents were sick of taking care of you." It was hard to argue with him because I felt like I was surrounded by dummies who had no grip on reality. The most that was expected of us was to wake up and doing exactly what I was told, which never set well with me. A valuable lesson I took from one of my favorite courses in college was to never be comfortable. Comfort allows no room for growth. "Comfort is the enemy of progress." When you're comfortable you become complacent. What progress could I gain from a senseless job? How could I capitalize off a stagnant lifestyle? The problem was I couldn't see past today, yet alone four years from now. Tomorrow held no value because each day brought no satisfaction. The individual I was now, rejected any and everything the army was built upon.

I stopped looking forward to the future because I was afraid that the army would just bring me more disappointment. In my mind, the idea of becoming an officer died soon after arriving in Arizona. I saw that they too were just errand boys and paper pushers, which was something I could never have forced myself to become.

Soon, I began to hear rumors. Funny looks were made; jokes were cracked but I never knew they were about me. I was so disconnected from everyone I had no clue what people were talking about. Everyone knew my name but I hardly knew anyone else's. I pretty much walked everywhere with my head down. Even though I wasn't paying attention to anything going on outside of my thoughts, it seemed like a lot of people were paying attention to me.

Especially SSG Brown, my platoon sergeant. We were the only platoon in my company that didn't go to Korea. He took charge of the remaining few, and we reported daily to him for instructions to be carried out during the workweek.

One particular day, I reported to PT on time but barely did any work, as usual. Like every other day, we gathered in formation around 1700 waiting to be dismissed to go home. SSG Brown took charge of the formation, put out some information regarding the next workday, and dismissed us. But, as he dismissed us, he called for me to stay behind to speak with him. This came as an utter surprise, because nobody typically noticed me outside of me getting into trouble. Therefore I assumed I'd done something wrong again and was about to face another punishment. But to my disbelief, he only wanted to talk.

Since my arrival, I hadn't gotten the proper chance to meet SSG Brown. He knew of me, just as everybody did, because of my infamous demeanor and behavior. Instead of scolding me about something I'd done, he insisted I relax and see him as a man, not as a sergeant, but a regular guy I could talk to. He was my superior, therefore customs and courtesies required me to address him as such. But he insisted we drop the army charades in order to have a normal conversation. He expressed his concerns with my behavior, saying he had been observing me since I arrived on base.

He broke the ice with, "What's wrong with you?" He skirted around the idea that I was having family or girlfriend troubles back home. But I laughed off his skepticism and insisted nothing was wrong with me.

"Since there's nothing wrong, tell me what I can do for you?" SSG Brown said.

Confused and hesitant I replied, "What do you mean?"

"What can I do to help make you be the best soldier you can be here at Fort Huachuca?"

Still confused, I tried to come up with something to say, but before I could get a word out SSG Brown stopped me, "I'm trying to keep you from getting kicked out of the army because that's where you're heading. What's wrong with you? Are you home sick? Having girlfriend troubles? What's wrong? How can I help you, because I can tell something's wrong with you."

In disbelief that he was still poking at the idea that a girlfriend back home was what was causing me such distress, I smirked and shook my head, "There's nothing wrong, sergeant."

"If there's nothing then wrong why can't you get with the program? They're not going to tolerate this behavior from you much longer." He pointed toward the commander and first sergeant's office as he said this. "You know that right?"

I nodded my head in agreement. He cut right to the point and came out and asked me, "What if I told you I could get you out of here in—"

I stopped him mid-sentence, knowing what he was about to say. I didn't want a way out. I never once thought about getting out. This whole time I've tried countless ways I could make this better for me, but never a way out. I loved to flirt with the idea of getting out the army but I knew I signed a contract and there was no way around that, so I thought.

"No no no, please don't finish that sentence," I insisted.

"Let me finish," SSG. Brown insisted. "What if I told you I could get you out of here in ninety days with an honorable discharge?"

"Wait. What? How?" I stammered in disbelief.

"I believe I can pull a few strings. I've done it once before with a soldier that desperately wanted out of the army. Just as I got him out, I can get you out. It's either that or you get your shit together and conform to the army's standards. Otherwise, I'm coming down hard on you if you keep up the behavior you've been displaying. I'll give you time to think it over. But once we start the process, there's no turning back. So I need you to make sure you make the right decision. I'll give you until Monday to give me an answer."

It was a Wednesday when SSG Brown pulled me aside to give me the second biggest decision I was going to make in my life so far. I had until Monday to decide what I wanted to do. I was nervous, excited, and for once I was giddy with joy. I'm not sure if I was happy that I was getting a way out of this hell hole, or if I was just happy that I could finally use my mind to make a decision of my own. Either way, I was overjoyed and had a lot to contemplate in a short amount of time.

CHAPTER 13
Self Realization

After talking with my platoon sergeant, I rushed back to the barracks, happier than ever before. My mind was working a million miles per hour. I was in total shock that this opportunity just fell out of the sky. I needed to calm down and pray and ask God for a sound mind and a clear heart before going forth with deciding on what to do. After praying, I called up my mother, my brother, my sister, my dog, even my cat—I called everyone that mattered to me. I needed their honest opinions on what I should do. I didn't want to make a hasty decision just because I was unhappy. I know not to make important decisions when my emotions are high. This decision had to be smart and strategic, just as I thought it was when I decided to join.

I included everyone in on this because I thought they would've made it easier for me to decide. But also because, when I first decided to join, so many people were hurt that I hid the decision from them. So I dialed everyone in my inner circle.

Within a few hours of calling around, everyone pretty much said the same thing, "It's your life, make the best decision you think would suit you." My mother, grandmother, and brother agreed I would ultimately live with the benefits or consequences, so they left it up for me to decide. Typically I seek their advice in hopes of hearing what they would do, and then decide if I agreed with their decision or not. This time they didn't give me that option. Each of them left it in my hands to decide. What I really needed was for them to make sense of either option, and after talking with each of them, I felt no closer to one side or the other. So I called my grade school best friend, Kalyn, someone who knows me inside and out.

Kalyn brought up a valid point throughout our conversation. She knew I was torn and needed help. Just as I did before asking for help, she sought out God. She narrowed it down to one question, "What have you been praying for?"

Since boot camp, I had prayed for peace and understanding from God. I needed peace in my heart to continue working a job I hated. I was so uneasy thinking I was going to waste four years of my life on a pointless job. On top of that, I ultimately needed to understand why I was in the army to begin with. She asked if I had ever prayed for a way out of the army, and I hadn't, not once. Throughout everything and the way I felt towards the army, I never seriously thought about actually trying to get out. Kalyn suggested that this was God's way of granting me peace and understanding of a real purpose outside the army. My heart desired to leave the army but my mind continued to rationalize the situation. Kalyn understood that sometimes God grants the desires of our hearts without ever praying for it. Which made a lot of sense. I locked that nugget of knowledge in my head and phoned one of friends from college friend, Jared A.

We met freshman year and getting to know him I understood that, in crucial times, he always knew how to decide what was best for him. He never really put himself in harm's way because he always thought of himself first, and I admired that. We talked often and he'd listened to me go on and on about how much I hated the army and how unhappy I was. If anybody knew the way I was feeling it was him. And, when I called him, instead of me asking him what I should do he basically told me. He knew I wasn't the same Tamarcus he met in college. During our calls he sensed there was something wrong long before I could tell him about my day at work. Every day it was something new, something worse than the day before.

He told me, "Friend, your mental health comes before anything. If you aren't happy, how do you expect to live like that? You can't play with your mental health Tamarcus."

His words rang loud and clear in my ears. But that wasn't quite enough to conjure up a decision just yet. There was one more person I had to consult before I made my mind up.

Me. Myself and I. I needed to listen to myself. What did I want? Did I want out? What was I going to do once I got out? Was I going to regret this decision later on in life? Was the army *really* as bad as I was making it out to be? What would the rest of my family think of me for quitting?

There was so much going on in my head at once I couldn't think straight. I was afraid to commit to a decision. I didn't want to make the wrong decision, again. I knew the easy answer was yes, to get me out of here as quick as possible! But the easier choice isn't always the best choice. It all came down to one last conversation with my dad's mom. I'd already spoken to her about what SSG Brown offered me, and she suggested I stay in the service. She knew the opportunities that could come by staying in, so she opted with the safest route. But I challenged her with the harder route. Just like I had questions for myself, she had questions for me also. She wondered, what if I took his offer? Where was I going to live? Where was I going to work? So much had changed in my life while my mom was at a stand still. I had no clue what was coming next. It scared her, but it didn't scare me. This became a pivotal point in my life. This felt like a second chance at the life I wanted after college. Only this time, had money saved up and a mind full of ideas.

Never before had I realized my true potential. I was equipped with a degree from a prestigious black institution of higher learning. Taught by renowned professors and doctors, I held the key to my success all along. But it wasn't until now that I knew I had it in me all along. There was so much doubt in my mind as to what I could accomplish after college. I was afraid of the real world. I knew I had to grow up and face adulthood, but I thought I wasn't ready. So I joined the army. One, I had no place to live and I wasn't sure I had what it took to land a job in corporate America. It took almost a year from graduating college to realize the entire time I was the only one holding myself back from success. It wasn't my mom, and it wasn't the army, it was me. Self-doubt and fear deterred me from making a smart decision.

Like I stated before, the easier choice isn't always the best choice. At the time, the army was actually the easier choice. It seemed hard because it was something I'd never done before, but it doesn't take a genius to join and get through the army. And if you keep your head down and do what they tell you, the checks come right in.

I knew I had more to offer the world than what the army required of me. I anticipated the stress of the real world, I anticipated finding a new purpose in life, I anticipated bills and rent, I anticipated any and everything to go wrong, but I knew I had what it took to overcome any obstacle. Also, I knew if I stayed in the army, at this rate, I'd probably get kicked out with a dishonorable discharge. So I waited eagerly for Monday to tell SSG Brown, "I want out!"

CHAPTER 14

March

The process began. No one knew but SSG Brown, the company commander, and me. It was to stay that way until I was given a definite date of discharge. I wasn't sure exactly how the process worked, but I kept my mouth shut and waited for the day to come.

Ninety days. Three months. I wanted to celebrate the victory but I couldn't help but feel defeated. I was still here. I wasn't gone yet. I was still a soldier. I was still a 25Q (a button pusher), and I still had to report to the damn motor pool for motor pool maintenance. Nothing had changed but a conversation with my sergeant. It was all just an adrenaline rush. A few weeks had gone by since I took the deal. I was extremely happy that I was getting out, but when? In May? In June? That was too far away and there wasn't much talk about me getting out after that. SSG Brown never officially gave me a date for anything. I just knew 90 days, but was it going to take so long? Was this what purgatory felt like? I needed to be grateful and be patient, so I tried.

That was until I found out we'd be gearing up for a field training exercise that would last for two weeks towards the middle of March. Here I was, Mr. Lucky, given the rare opportunity to break my four-year contract and return to sweet civilian life. But first I had to go play army in the middle of nowhere for two long ass weeks. I quickly lost sight of what was promised to me, and reality sucked back in. The reality was that I was still apart of the US Army, property of the US government.

By mid-March, I'd forgotten all about my secret deal with SSG Brown. I was far tot focused on dreading sleeping outside for the next two weeks. The field was boring and cold. Winter hadn't yet subsided, and the desert nights of Arizona were far colder than the day. Two weeks seemed like a month of doing mostly nothing. Field exercises are meant as mock deployments. Basically, all you have is your equipment, gear, and whatever else you could fit in your rucksack to keep you entertained for the next fourteen days.

The field was another learning opportunity for me to truly understand how much I hated the army. However, although I hated every bit of it, I was impressed by how smooth the entire operation carried out.

In the first few days, we grounded our equipment and set up communications. If you've ever watched a war movie and wondered how soldiers in the middle of nowhere were able to use laptops and make calls, know that it's my MOS that makes that possible. By deploying satellites and configuring radios, we're able to provide Internet and wireless calling in a remote area. Maybe it sounds exciting to you, but in actuality the equipment runs itself for the most part. My job is to ground the equipment, hook up the cables, push a series of buttons, and bam, WiFi and mobile connection. The rest of my job is to ensure the generators don't run out of fuel and the connections don't fail. Ultimately, push a few buttons, find a signal, and sit around hoping the connections never go down. Most of the work is unloading and loading the endless boxes and poles and heavy equipment. We really weren't told to do much but just stay awake and maintain connectivity. I know, easy money right? What's sweeter than getting paid to sit on your butt all day? In reality, it's not caked up to be all what you might think, unless comfort eases your mind.

This was not life. Life is prosperous and fulfilling. In life you have to work hard for the things you earn. Everything by this point was given to me, or I got it with little to no effort. The paycheck that hit my account twice a month wasn't earned money. I didn't do anything meaningful. I only halfway did what I was told and collected an easy check. I felt like I was robbing taxpayers of their hard earned money, which never sat right with me. There were tons of soldiers I encountered who loved the army, who desired to serve their country, even die for their country. I was just there for the benefits. Which many others were too, but they did their jobs and I didn't. I got by. I didn't care about my battle buddies, I wasn't excited about deployments like everyone else, and I could care less who scored the highest on their PT test. I didn't fit in. This life wasn't for me and it was eating at my mind everyday that I was somewhere where I didn't belong, doing something I hated doing.

Instead of trying to live up to the hype of a disciplined soldier, I took the deal presented to me in order to shape my life the way I saw fit. While in the field, dreaming of the day where I would no longer be in the army, I searched for jobs. We had our phones and snacks, so I balled up in my cot and searched for a new start. It would eventually hit me that soon enough I wouldn't wake up and have to lace up my boots and wear the uniform anymore. The army only provided me with one perspective, whereas the real world provides one with multiple perspectives in which reality lies. I wanted, needed to be apart of reality. Not pretend to be GI Joe.

CHAPTER 15
Mental Evaluation

Two days before the field exercise was over, I was snatched from our FOB and started my out-processing. I returned all of my issued gear and equipment, still without a specific date when I was going to be released. I knew the day was coming because I'd started visiting the different agencies on base that help transition soldiers back into civilian life, which is brutally different than army life. The transition phase is designed to be a form of rehabilitation. The effects of living an active duty lifestyle can be crippling when rejoining civility. These soldiers are solely dependent on the army and the Department of Defense, and it's up to them to restore a soldier back to their former self before returning to the real world. Despite the efforts, I believe no soldier returns to civility the same as when they enlisted. The army changes you, some for the better, some for the worse.

Much is required to be a part of active duty. It's mentally, physically, and emotionally draining to keep up with the everyday life of a soldier. It deeply affects the relationships you have with your family. The army's priorities always come before your own, your ego must always be put aside, and that alone can take a toll on someone's mental capabilities. Active duty for sure had taken a toll on my mind, but I'd never before shared with anyone how deep the burden of being in the army lied within.

April 27, 2018, SSG Brown escorted me to the mental health facility on the second floor of the hospital on base at Fort Huachuca. I hadn't given much thought about the appointment with a psychiatrist. The only thing I couldn't think of was a doctor hooking a bunch of wires to my head and asking me a series of questions while he looked at scribbles printing out from an EKG. Of course, that wasn't the case.

SSG Brown and I walked to the receptionist desk, he checked me in and the receptionist handed me a laptop. She instructed me to have a seat in the waiting area and fill out the survey on the laptop. SSG Brown ensured I was ok and told me he'd be downstairs in the lobby waiting if I needed him.

I opened the laptop and saw that the survey was questions pertaining to my everyday life, thoughts, attitudes and behaviors. The further I got along in the survey, the more deep and intimate the questions got. I would soon figure out the questions in that survey were just the tip of the iceberg.

"Tamarcus Lott." A deep, husky male's voice called out as the door from the waiting room leading into the back of the mental facility opened. I looked up to find a heavyset white man, honestly resembling Santa Clause, well Kris Kringle. To my surprise, he was a civilian. I was expecting an army specialist, but instead it was Santa.

As soon as we entered his office, the questions began. The doctor asked how long I'd been in the army, which he followed up with what was causing me to get out so soon? By now, only a year had passed since I swore allegiance to the army. Which introduced the never-ending story of searching for my place in the army.

"Wrong job, wrong branch, wrong person," I explained. "This just isn't for me." Apparently my answer wasn't good enough because he kept poking around as to why I wanted out after only being in for only a year.

"What's the real problem?" The doctor asked.

"I told you, I don't like my job. It's just not for me."

The doctor explained, "We all work jobs we don't like. But that doesn't mean you get to just up and quit because you don't like something. There will be plenty more things in life you don't like. Will you run from all of your problems when it gets to hard for you? I'm just checking to make sure this is something you've truly thought through, and you're not just going to quit every time a job gets hard."

He was kind of sassy to look a lot like Santa Clause, but of course he had no clue that I'd been depressed since the day I joined. How could he have known what I was feeling? I didn't want to confess to him everything I'd been feeling for so long. I was embarrassed, and I didn't want to seem crazy or unfit for discharge. He was asking all of the questions I knew the rest my family and friends would ask when they got word I was no longer in the military.

Evading his questions, I just shook my head, shrugged my shoulders, and said, "I'm unhappy."

The doctor asked with great concern, "What's making you so unhappy?" He even sat up in his chair waiting to hear what I had to say.

My head dropped in shame. I could only shake my head and hide my face. I began to get teary eyed. I tried my best not to blink, knowing if I did the tears swelling up in my eyes would start to fall. The question echoed in my head, "What's making you so unhappy?" It triggered all the emotions I was bottling up from the moment I stepped off the plane until now. Silence filled the room.

The doctor sat patiently waiting for my answer. And I sat for a while without saying a word, head bowed.

He had no clue what I'd been going through, how I really felt. All of the emotions from basic training, AIT, and now here at my unit all of sudden made my heart feel tremendously heavy.

From day one I tried to make this decision work for me. I thought I could swallow my pride and accomplish what I once thought was impossible. What my family thought was impossible. I knew this decision was made circumstantially; I had nowhere else to turn to in hopes of a better future. My mom had her own problems to deal with, and I was of an age where I knew I couldn't rely on her anymore. I thought I made the decision a man would make when his back was against the wall. But my decision only led me down a path of deeper agony. I hated everything about the army: the food, the culture, the people, the senseless workload, and the endless ridiculous orders I had to obey. There was never an escape. I resorted to sleeping pills after I gave up drinking every night. The effects of drinking were far too harsh to deal with the next morning, so I found pills that would help me sleep. Anytime I was alone in my room, I popped those pills. I didn't want to be alert and awake because literally everything around me reminded me that I had four more years of living like this. There were nights before I went to bed when I thought what if I didn't wake up the next morning? What if I just disappeared? What if I took all those sleeping pills? There were multiple times I thought death was the solution. Life was weighing down heavy on my shoulders. I needed an escape. I couldn't think of a way out because I signed the dotted line that kept me bound to this life for four years. I was certain dying was the easier route. If I took a handful of pills, all of my problems would vanish. Pills, pills pills. Before being approached by SSG Brown, I was increasingly thinking of ways to commit suicide. A gun, pills, hanging myself, anything to rob me of this feeling.

By this time my uniform pants were on the verge of being soaked. I still hadn't spoken a word. I just thought of all the reasons why I was unhappy. All the while, the doctor just sat and watched me cry while I drowned myself in regret. The tears fell like raindrops. Heavy and hard. They wouldn't let up. I couldn't stop crying. I found the place I kept avoiding, it was like the "sunken place."

He broke the silence, "What is it Tamarcus? Something has you deeply emotional and it won't go away unless you talk about it."

I swallowed so hard I almost choked. My mouth was so dry from crying so hard. I tried to explain my tears, "I wasn't made for this. No, it's not hard. Everybody thinks this is to hard for me but it's not! It's just not what I was made for. I went to college for four years to learn about how I was going to be on TV one day. Nothing I'm doing is setting me up for that future. I hate it here! I hate everybody here!"

I stopped myself and I paused. I took a moment to catch my breath and attempt to calm down. I had gotten so caught up in my own passion and anger, I'd forgotten who I was talking to. I was far too deep in my feelings to realize I'd just poured my heart out to this doctor, who could possibly deem me mentally unstable for discharge. Suicide is taken seriously in the army and I knew they wouldn't release me had they known I was potentially suicidal. So I stopped myself before I said something I couldn't take back.

"It's clear you're unhappy with the army, it's actually pathetic how sad you are. Never before has a soldier broke down like that before because he was unhappy with a job. Usually I get the ones who are homesick or battling other personal issues. This is a first and I'm not going to get in the way of giving you what you what, honestly what you need." The doctor stopped talking, he handed me a box of tissues, wrote notes on his notepad, and that was that. He handed me a packet of papers to give to SSG Brown. Before I reached the lobby where he was waiting, I took a peek inside of the packet to see what the therapist wrote on the mental evaluation form.

Service member has no desire to serve. Serving will cause detriment to service member and to his unit. Service member mental status is sustainable for discharge.

Signed Dr. Santa Clause

CHAPTER 16

May

On May 1, 2018, I was HONORABLY discharged from the United States Army.

It was like seeing the sun for the first time after doing a hard nine years in prison. I felt freer then ever before.

Immediately following the appointment for my mental evaluation, my commander received my clearing papers for me to officially be discharged out of the military. As he took out a large red folder that read "PVT LOTT", he jokingly asked if I'd changed my mind and gave me one last chance to turn back before I signed my discharge papers. Before he could finish his joke my eyes got real big and I barked out a loud, "No," and and nearly snatched the pen and papers out of his hand.

That was the first joke I'd heard in a long time that actually made smile and laugh. Just the thought of him thinking I would change my mind made me chuckle. My commandeer stopped and said, "Wow, you know that's the first I've ever seen this guy crack a smile."

His comment made me stop and realized that the people I had been surrounded by for the past six months had never seen me do something that I used to be known for: smiling and laughing. But it was all behind me, and I knew I'd be smiling a lot more once I cleared the base.

After I officially signed my life back over to the Lord, life started picking up really fast. I waited around for months like a sitting duck for a date to fall out of thin air, and just like that May 1st fell out of the sky.

Night after night in the field I applied and called jobs around the country. I was open to moving anywhere. I didn't need a company to pay for the move because the army was moving me at their expense to wherever I decided to settle and call home. The entire country was at my leisure. Honestly, this felt too perfect, and the thought hit me that this was what I was supposed to be feeling at the end of college. My mind was free to roam about the endless possibilities that were out there for me. California and Colorado were my top two states I wanted to live. But the cost of living and the job competition was setting me up for a gamble I wasn't ready to take coming straight out of the army.

I applied to a ton of jobs in the communications field: administrative assistant, junior level communications director, marketing specialists, and many more. I even convinced my command team to let me take a few days off to go on job interviews. They agreed, but the farthest I could travel had to be within a radius of 250 miles.

Tucson and Phoenix were the closest big cities within that radius, so I applied heavily for jobs throughout Phoenix and eventually got called back to set up an interview with a small upcoming marketing firm. I took my leave and headed to Phoenix. The interview went great, but just as I was getting in my car to head back to base a public relations firm in Dallas emailed with interest in my resume for a communications position for which they were hiring.

Dallas was thirteen hours from Fort Huachuca. I was nervous even looking at the email because the realization of moving thirteen hours away was daunting. But of course, I opened the email, which asked me to schedule a preliminary over-the-phone interview. After my phone interview was completed, they asked me to come to Dallas to interview with them in person.

At first I was thinking no way I was going to Dallas because I had to stay within my 250 miles range. But I still had days off from work, and I had the money for the trip. I thought, "What hell could they do to me, and how would they even find out?"

I scheduled the in-person interview in Dallas, but of course, I wasn't going to drive thirteen hours to Dallas for one interview. I applied to more jobs in the city in hopes of scheduling two more interviews. I managed to set up another interview with another company. So I drove all the way to Dallas with my suits pressed and ready to go. When I got there the interviews went great and I already had an email offering the job in Phoenix. All three companies were impressed enough to offer me a position, all to start immediately following my discharge from the army. I'd just finished my final interview in Dallas which offered my a position on the spot. Just as I was pulling out of the parking lot when the previous job I interview for offered me a position. I had to stop driving and park the car because I couldn't see for the tears that voluntarily formed in my eyes. I called my grandma Bettie to share the news with her. Had I not took a breath to calm down I would've been hysterically crying. I was beyond convinced I wasted and erased four years of my life. Nothing made sense to me and I was lost in sadness and gave up on my future. But God smiled on me, reassuring me that I still have what it takes to make my dreams come true.

Proactively, I took the time in both Phoenix and Dallas to look at apartments and try to get a feel for each city. It was hard making a decision on what job to take and which city to live in because it was all so surreal. I was scared to make a choice. Three job offers in two different cities? Me? I did that? How?

I discovered a new flame burning in the pit of my stomach. It fueled this new strong feeling of ambition. I was hopeful again and it felt so damn good. I was starting to feel more like my old self.

Not being in the right headspace made the entire past year feel like a complete out of body experience. From the moment I got that text from my mom saying she'd been evicted out of her apartment up until my discharge, it all felt like a dream. Or really, a nightmare.

Every day I woke up and I couldn't believe what I was doing. I found myself shaking my head in disbelief at what was my life. I watched myself nearly lose my mind. I was aware of it all. I saw myself become a completely different person. I gave up on everything, there was nothing left for me to believe in. The scariest thing I ever experienced was accepting defeat. Accepting that things wouldn't get better created such a dark space in my mind. I walked with no purpose, I thought with no purpose. Even though I heard it since I was kid that, "Life happens." And I knew life got in the way of so many people's dreams, but I couldn't accept it getting in the way of mine.

I can't say I had hope things would eventually change for me in the army. I can't say I believed I would've snapped out of it and made it through all four years. SSG Brown caught me in a deep rut of depression and self-pity, he lent me a hand out of that rut and I truly owe him the world. Because of him, I knew that tomorrow would be better. I was sure I had seen my darkest days. I thought that no feeling could be worse than wanting to disappear. I thought I knew what it took to finally make shit happen for myself. I was finally ready to put my degree to use!

HOMELESS

CHAPTER 17
New Apartment

Even though I wanted to give a proper goodbye to SSG Brown and a few other soldiers I developed relationships with, I ended up packing up my car and leaving in the middle of the night without saying a word. I gassed up and hopped on the highway a little before midnight. I didn't have to be out of the barracks until late the next day, but I was ready to close this chapter of my life. I tried sleeping in my room one last night, but my mind was restless.

I started down the highway in complete silence. I started off with praying to God, asking grace and mercy and thanking him for my freedom. If I tried to explain the joy I felt in that moment, I would do nothing but stammer, stutter, and start smiling uncontrollably. I was "tickled pink," as my mom used to say. I couldn't thank God enough that that I was out of the army. I sighed in relief over and over again the entire thirteen hours to Dallas.

First thing on the agenda was to find an apartment. I tried at one apartment complex but the endless emailing and calling over the phone was too much of a hassle for them to handle and they decided to wait and call me while I was on the road to Dallas. They denied my application because my new job hadn't confirmed my income after multiple attempts to reach them. I almost panicked because I was reassured after my interview that the office would make my transition to Dallas go as smoothly as possible. I called the office and spoke with the guy who hired me and hammered him with a million questions as to why my income wasn't verified with the leasing office when they called. He calmed me down by emailing the job offer letter and expected salary. That was all cool, but I still didn't have a place to stay. I pulled over to a rest stop to book a hotel for the next two days because I only had the weekend to search the city for an apartment.

I checked into my hotel early Wednesday, around noon. As soon as I got in the room, I dropped my bags and started searching on my phone for vacant apartments around the city. I called a few and told them I was on the way to look at the properties. Only to make matters more chaotic, it was pouring down raining the entire day. I spent the entire day in and out of my car trying to look at apartments only to be told I could move in next week or two weeks from now. I needed to move in by that Saturday. After driving to three different apartment complexes around Dallas, I finally found a place to call my new home. The downside was it was in an urban area. I wanted to stay on the Northside of Dallas, the newer developing area. But the rent was less than the initial apartment I looked at, and there was a move-in special. Most importantly they were able to move me in on Friday. This time I had all of the necessary paperwork I need to qualify for the lease. All I had to do was cough up the money.

Less than twenty-four hours from being discharged from the army, I had moved to a new state, a new city, and secured a one bedroom apartment all on my own, at twenty three years old. The depressing days of basic training and the agonizing time in AIT all vanished at the turn of a key into my new apartment. The independence I longed for as a child was now a living reality. I was officially on my own.

Even though my apartment was on the third floor and faced the highway, it was the perfect size and quiet. New black stainless appliances, newly renovated, I was itching to decorate and furnish the place. My first time seeing the place I thought, "This is where I'm going to live for the next year, at least. My next birthday will be spent here." I was so proud of myself for making this big leap of faith. I was under my own roof, I could walk around naked, wash the dishes when I felt like it, and I could sing as loud as I wanted to in the shower! "I pay the bills up in this b*** and what I say goes," I yelled at my imaginary kids. I waited all these years to say what my mom nagged us about throughout my teenage years.

There wasn't much for me to move up the three flights of stairs, except my 55" flatscreen TV. Other than that, it was just lugging all my clothes upstairs. I settled in fast. I made a trip to Walmart and Target to stock up on toiletries, groceries, and an air mattress. I figured I would "rough it" until I had the money to buy a mattress and a frame. I didn't have any WiFi or cable, and the cell phone service was complete trash, so the first night in my apartment was quiet and pretty boring. I cooked myself dinner and sat on the floor in my living room and couldn't have been any happier—I wasn't in the army anymore!

At this point, I thought about my life a lot. The army really opened my eyes to things I didn't realize about myself. From not talking as much, I really got to know myself on a deeper level. I had a stronger sense of what I wanted out of life now. I had seen so many people fall short of their dreams because they got caught up in a cycle of bad habits or bad choices. Life is unimaginably hard, but it's still doable. I'm known to be a persistent person, I've dealt with a lifetime of chaos and setbacks, but I've never lost the will to keep going. The army almost dimmed that light, but something, or someone, intervened. The universe was showing me that I had a purpose. I'd been given a second chance at this thing called life and I'd be a fool to ignore it. Someone is in my ear was telling me that I could finally do all the crazy things I came up with in my head. It was like someone was nudging my spirit and saying, "Do it." I was ready to do infinity and beyond but, I asked God to humble me first and foremost.

CHAPTER 18

New me, New Job, Who dis?

On the morning of May 7, 2018, I began my first day as an entry-level public relations associate for a marketing firm, which was located on the outskirts of downtown Dallas. This was more than a start-up company; it was an established marketing company for a few Fortune 500 companies. Their clientele was impressive and their operations were precise and professional.. I chose this company over the others because I saw an opportunity to establish myself with experienced career professionals that could potentially help me grow in my profession.

Instead of wasting time with pointless orientation sideshows welcoming me to the company, I got right to work. I was taught key marketing tips and tools. Members of the company led meetings every morning in the form of "teach-backs." On Monday mornings, the executives taught a lesson and at random the following morning someone else from the office would teach back the lesson. This was exciting for me seeing the high level executives being so personable and accessible with the employees of the office. In a short amount of time, I learned and gained new tools that I will carry with me for the rest of my career.

But like every job, this one had its perks and its downfalls. For instance, being the only black guy in the entire office was definitely a downfall. Truly, it hadn't dawned on me that I was working in an office full of white people, as I never focused on race, until one morning one of the executives told the guy training me to pull me to the side and address the fact that I didn't have on a blazer. The dress code was explained to me before I accepted the position, therefore I was already familiar with this rule. I explained to the hiring manager that, because I came straight from the army, most of my business attire was back home in Memphis and I couldn't afford to buy a new suit at the time.

She reassured me that I would be given time to adjust before being hassled about the rules. My trainer, Dave, offered to let me borrow his blazer until I had the money to buy one for myself, which would've been a great idea if he weren't twice my size. I insisted it wouldn't fit, but he insisted I needed one "per the dress code." The next morning he met me in the parking garage with the blazer. Not only was it nearly three sizes too big, it wasn't black nor was it navy or any other professional color. It was a two-toned pink and light blue paisley patterned blazer. Honestly, It looked like a suit a black old-school Baptist pastor would wear on Easter Sunday. Thanking Dave for the hideous blazer, I draped it over my arm, but he insisted I had to wear it before walking into the building.

This had to be the most humiliating experience of my life. There I was in front of the company executives and about thirty other company employees with a giant coat swallowing my whole body. I tried to focus and take notes on what was being taught, but I couldn't help but focus on how much I looked and felt like a fool. Every morning I tried to compensate for not having a blazer by over dressing with the clothes I did have. I made sure I had on a nice watch, a tie with a tie clip, strong contrasting socks, just for it all to be swallowed under an ugly paisley embroidered overcoat. I had to wear it every morning during the morning meetings. I felt like the "ugly broke black kid."

I know for certain I dress better and present myself better than the average guy, so it was hard for me to accept the fact that I looked like a complete clown in a professional environment, all because of a dumb dress code. In hindsight, I could've been blowing things out of proportion and just swallowed my pride and wore his blazer like a big boy.

However, I found myself wanting to ball-up and die when the CEO of the company and the board members from out of town visited our branch and saw me in that blazer. They all noticed me, but not for my work ethic. They saw me as the black guy in the office who looked like a jackass. But I digress, because no matter how I felt in that moment it would never top the way I felt in the army. So I dealt with it and tried to outshine the ugly blazer with my work ethic.

CHAPTER 19
May 15, 2019

After living the corporate, big city lifestyle for two weeks, I came to the conclusion that I loved Dallas and my new apartment, but I hated my job. It was not at all what I expected it to be. I was not cut out to be a public relations associate.

I didn't hate the entire job as a whole; it had its perks. I chose this company over the other two because I saw room for personal growth within this company. This is still true today, but the work itself was not at all what was explained in the interview. There was a "field" portion of training that I wasn't discussed or misunderstood. This was unexpected and confused me about my official job role. But, I was stuck selling products for our clients in unconventional was. I wasn't depressed that the job didn't turn out to be my dream job, but I was bummed out that I didn't find any enjoyment in what I did. Regardless of how I felt, I now had bills to pay. I had to wake my butt up every morning for a paycheck.

Life hadn't slowed down much since leaving Arizona. The hours at the office were long, the same hours as in the army, but I wasn't moving around like I was on base. I was always tired because we were just sitting around in the mornings for meetings and selling products for clients in the evenings. It took some time for me to adjust to this type of work.

I could have cared less that I didn't like my new job. This wasn't the army and I could quit whenever I pleased. The only thing that was causing me to worry was that my savings account was near empty and my checking account wasn't looking any better. I was briefed before separating from the army that I would receive my last paycheck on May fifteenth. I woke up that morning and nothing was deposited into my account. My first full paycheck from my new job wouldn't be until sometime in June. By then, I would have completely ran out of money.

The following week, instead of receiving the huge payday I'd been expecting from the army, I came home to a letter in the mail from the United States Treasury attempting to collect the remainder of a debt of $3,198. Along with that letter was another thanking me for a payment of $3,892. In other words, the government garnished my last check from the army, covering the first installment of the bonus that paid out when I initially arrived to my unit.

Unused days of paid leave, travel allowances, and half a month's pay was all in that last check I was waiting for, approximately $4,000. Before leaving Fort Huachuca, I saved up a large amount of money to sustain me until I received the last bit of money from the army. I knew I was going to have to pay my bonus back, but in the transition back to a civilian, no one mentioned they would garnish my last check.. Not only was I running out of money, but my next paycheck wasn't coming for a month's time. I was hired in the middle of a pay period and my first full check was a whole month away and that check wouldn't be a reflection of what I'd actually be paid on average. During "field training" we were paid a training rate, upon completion I would then start receiving my discussed salary. Despite knowing I would be selling things in the field, I knew the pay offset and difference. When I initially accepted the job this wasn't a concern because I anticipated the final lump sum from the army.

This really changed the course of everything. I didn't have enough money without the big payout from the army to make it another month working this job. I had no clue how I would pay for gas for my car, the energy bill, rent, and other new expenses I planned to pay with that money.

Something had to give. The cost of moving started to take its toll fast. I didn't bother finding out if the company was going to pay to relocate me because the army was paying my final move. Some of the money used for moving was paid upfront but the large sum of it would be paid out once I completed the necessary paperwork. That money also was lost due to the bonus repayment.. There was no way I was going to keep up, financially, with work, living twenty-five minutes away from the office, having money for food, phone bill, and a car note.

I was forced to quit. Maybe it wasn't the best decision at the time, but I had no choice. I couldn't afford to continue commuting and working this job for the next month without any payment. I needed to find a job where I could make quick cash.

After I quit, I wasn't getting calls to set up interviews, instead of knocking it out of the park like last time, I was repeatedly told that I was a great candidate but lacked the experience. Nearly fresh out of college, I was stuck trying to figure out what experience I could have if I was applying to an entry level position? Days turned into weeks without a job. Part-time jobs in retail and waiting tables were my last resort, when they should've been the first resort. Ignorantly, I applied to office positions and areas I had minimum experience. I was surviving off of family and friends sending me ten and twenty dollars here and there to eat and keep my lights and water on in my apartment.

Life was starting to swallow me whole, but I couldn't have been in a happier place in my life. There was one major positive that kept lingering throughout my head that kept me happy: I wasn't in the army anymore. This thought alone brought a bright and wide smile across my face. Life was raining down relentlessly on my head. But, I felt no stress, no pressures. I knew things were bad and I was at risk of being put out on the street, but deep down I was happy because I was no longer in the dark depressing confines of the army. Yet again life wasn't going my way but this time I embraced it, accepting it rather than shying away and worrying about things I couldn't control. What I could control I tried to change, what I couldn't, I gave it to God. I kept my composure throughout my struggles. I understand more than anything that life is a process and all things pass in due season. This was only a season and I needed to weather the storm. If only I knew how bad the storm would get.

Over the next two months, I depleted my entire checking and savings accounts. Just about all of my closest family and friends had given me money to keep me afloat during this time of need. Not realizing how long this employment drought would last, I cut back on everything that required money. Money was running so low I intuitively picked up old habits from undergrad. I washed my clothes by hand. I didn't have money for groceries so I ate ramen noodles daily, and stretched every single dollar I had. I'd been in this situation before, struggling to pay bills and struggling to pay for food.

Somehow in undergrad I could stretch twenty dollars to pay for a week of meals. My friends and I used resources around campus to help get us by when we didn't have much money. Free food, free drinks, free anything we were pretty much there. Just like college offered free stuff on occasion, I was certain there had to be someone out there that could help me. Somehow I knew there were resources to help people in times like this. Community outreach, churches, charities, anybody could've helped me because I was damn near out of money and out of food.

I filled my tank up with the last of the money I had. I chose not to buy food with that last bit of cash, hoping desperately that a job would call and I could use the gas to drive to the interview. I trusted God to help me find a way out. Everyday I asked for guidance and understanding. He hadn't quite yet given me understanding as to why my life was spinning out of control, but he did give me some guidance. With the power of the Internet I found a local outreach center that established a food panty that distributed food to low-income families. I had no income, so I was sure I wouldn't be turned away. Only open on Thursdays, I had to wait two days for my next meal. I didn't eat for two days and it was ok. I didn't gripe, I didn't complain.

Thursday morning I woke up humbled. Never in a million years did I ever think that I'd be hundreds of miles away from home, alone in a new city with no money and no food to eat. I was sure there was somebody I could've called that would've sent me money had I told them I was starving and had no food in my fridge. But I got tired of asking.

Their yes's started to become no's and it was embarrassing calling people asking for money for something as simple as food. Now a grown man, with bills and responsibilities, I couldn't even fulfill one of the most basic human necessities. I'm appreciative of having family and friends that support me beyond belief, but I had to grow the hell up and take matters into my own hands. I desperately wanted to be self reliant and independent. My pride could've easily made visiting the food pantry a shameful experience, but I wouldn't allow it. This was a growing experience.

The women at the community center were nice and polite. Much like my grandmothers, they were sweet and loving, and it stunned them when they realized I was gathering groceries for myself. As young as I was, they didn't expect it. I made it clear to them it was for me and I was the one going home to cook it. The ladies bagged up some additional food for me to take home. Before I left, I hugged each of them and loaded the goods in my car. Before I could finish unloading the bags out of the cart my eyes began to water. I truly felt the love from them and appreciated that, although I was miles away from home, there were still good loving people around to help see others through their toughest times.

This was the first time I cried since leaving the army. These tears weren't from sadness but from joy. Not only because I was about to go home and eat a good ass meal, but I also felt that what I just experienced was a defining point in my life.

CHAPTER 20
July 2018

Everyday is a new opportunity for success, but success is a process. A lot of people tend to think that success happens overnight, that some big break will come and change everything. Success can also be as big as being the first man to land on the moon. Leading up to the moon landing, NASA and the US Government experienced a ton of failure, but in the end, they succeeded. The public rarely sees the process, though. We only glorify the event. But the process, sometimes, can be far more rewarding than the actual event.

I got a job delivering pizza. Domino's was one job along with a slew of others I applied to that would quickly hire me and put me to work. The pay wasn't much, which I knew going into it, but it was a start. I was more excited to start making tips at this job than I was the morning of my first day at my old job.

At this point, I was almost two months behind on rent, and the leasing office was only granting me a grace period because I served my country. It seemed like being a veteran was paying off more than actually being in the army. Rent for May was paid for along with the deposit, and I had just enough to pay for June, but I had nothing for the month of July. Before I left Arizona I paid a couple of months forward on my car note, but that was also about to be due in August.

Although I made a strategic plan to save money from delivering pizza to pay bills, that job alone wasn't going to keep me from getting evicted come August. The leasing office was closing in on my grace period, and I knew by the end of July I would need to pay for both the past month's rent as well as August's, my car bill, and every other bill that I neglected to pay. Shockingly, the only bills I didn't have to worry about were my students loans because they were still in deferment.

I continued hunting for a second job, and in the meantime I tried to sell all things I had of value: a 55" smart TV, a wireless Bluetooth speaker, Apple TV, an old iPhone 6s, all went up for sale online. I bagged a good portion of some nice clothes I owned to sell to Plato. Gradually all of it sold to cover everything except rent.

I stopped spiraling downward and got a grip on my life. At first I was very reluctant to sell my things. I was already sleeping on an air mattress—what good would it be to be in an apartment with no entertainment to take my mind off my situation? I realized my situation was only circumstantial. It was hard selling my things, but I realized I was being materialistic during a time where it didn't make sense to hold on to things that I would eventually be able to buy back once things got right again. What good was a TV if I had nowhere to live? They were just things.

Around this time, the end of July was creeping up. Rent was $860 a month, and with August fast approaching and July still unpaid, eviction seemed inevitable. I wasn't playing games with the leasing office, as most people do with their landlords. I kept it honest with management as soon as I fell behind after the first month. I tried to buy more time, hoping that if I worked open to close every day I'd be able get by.

While I tried working relentlessly, my mother called to tell me she'd be taking a trip with her pastor for a revival at a church right outside Dallas. She'd never been to Texas before, and I thought it was a coincidence that she'd be in for a trip to Texas as soon as I moved there. Still, it was something to look forward to. It was only for the weekend, enough for me to have lunch and spend time with her. She was completely oblivious to everything going on with me. We had talks over the phone when I first moved to Dallas but once everything started spiraling out of control I stopped calling. I saw that our conversations were mostly about how I was making ends meet without the money from the army. I wasn't complaining in hopes she would give me anything. I complained because that's what I was dealing with. I started to feel bad for her, knowing she couldn't do anything to help. I downplayed a lot of what I actually told my mom I was going through to ease her worrying. I knew now I was fully on my own and she was still dealing with her problems of her own. The most help my mom ever offered was to pray and told me to seek God. I knew that already and was definitely praying and asking God for help, so while I knew her intentions were good, there was little to nothing we were able to talk about, thus I quit calling all together.

Visiting with my mom and her pastor from Memphis was good for my spirit. The talks over dinner were encouraging and uplifting. What was rather disturbing was that my mom noticed I'd lost a bit of weight. In fact, the meal we had was probably the most filling meal I'd had for some time. I'd devoted my time to working and saving money. I barely ate because I didn't want to spend money on food. I was growing thin and it wasn't flattering knowing that I'd been skinny my whole life and now here I was, starving myself to make ends meet, and only making myself look skinnier.

After lunch we rode back to their hotel and talked a bit more before I left for work. As I got out of the car, without me asking for a cent, my mother gave me some money for gas.

Excited like it was Christmas I hugged my mom and left the hotel to fill up my tank. Just as I was pulling out of the hotel's driveway, another car cut me off, swiping the front end of my car and damaging the left side of my front bumper.

Blessed beyond measure, the damage wasn't serious and only damaged the bumper. But, to my serious detriment, not only did I not have the money to get my car fixed, I also didn't have car insurance. Ironically, my car insurance expired one week before having the wreck. Car insurance was simply something that I couldn't afford, as I was working so hard to just pay the most basic necessities. But no matter how hard I worked, I couldn't seem to get ahead. Why was this happening to me? Why were so many bad things happening to me? Everyday I seemed to hit a new low. The more I dealt with the more I started to think leaving the army was a bad idea.

CHAPTER 21

Homeless

What's the worst they can say? No? No was the worst thing that anybody could tell me at this point. I needed so much and asking those closest to me for help me was never easy. Shirking my pride, I asked away.

I don't know any millionaires. No one in my family is wealthy enough to consume the burdens of others without them too going under from carrying the responsibilities of someone else. But help can present itself in a number of ways. Through advice, networking, jobs, and relationships, any type of help from others can surely make a difference when you're going through tough times.

After enduring this hardship for long enough, I realized I couldn't do it all on my own, and the little help I was getting from family and friends—even though it meant the world to me—wasn't making much of a difference.

Extracurricular activities in college put me in rooms with a lot of successful prominent people. These were professionals who worked with some of the most powerful people in the world. One night, while I was sitting in my apartment and scrolling through my contacts, I found my last chance of hope.

There was one person I'd met and stayed in contact with outside of all throughout my time in college and afterward. He had access to jobs and people I dreamt of having access to. For sure, he also went through his fair share of struggles and would understand what I was going through.

Of course, he told me no to giving me any amount of money, but instead he wanted "point me in the direction I needed to go." I emailed him a copy of my resume hoping that he could connect me with people that would change the course of my career path. I didn't expect him to reply to my email saying, "I didn't realize the lack of experience you have in your field."

He suggested I focus on others jobs to get the money I desperately needed. Other than feeling humiliated for airing out my struggles to someone who couldn't help me, I simply felt defeated. I was on the verge of living out on the street and he offered me no help at all. His measly advice put a bad taste in my mouth.

His no would be the last no I needed to hear to stop asking anyone else for any advice or money. I couldn't understand how I was losing everything I so rightfully earned. Army life was over, it was behind me, but this new life I was creating for myself was under the influence of pain—the pain of being alone. Not alone in the sense of not having companionship with anyone in Dallas, but in the sense of being connected to so many people around the country but not one could really help me out of this situation. The only person I figured who could help me was me. Me and God.

I would say I weighed out all of my options before deciding to live in my car, but there weren't many options to weigh. Where was I going to go? Back to Memphis? In Memphis there were several couches I could sleep on, couches in homes that weren't mine. If I took that route, there would've been a lingering pressure from someone else to get off their couch and get my shit together. I didn't need that. I provided myself with enough guilt and perseverance to get my own shit together. Having a friend or loved one threatening to put me out after so many months would only ruin the very relationship that allowed me to sleep under their roof in the first place.

Living in my car seemed more and more ideal versus asking to live with someone else. I paid up a few months on my car note before leaving the army and could save up money while I planed my next move. An average person would find it absurd to live in a car. Instead of seeing this as a defeat, I recognized living in my car as a reminder of how bad I wanted to be successful and independent.

Once the leasing office started leaving letters and final notices, I pretty much accepted the fact that I was going to lose my apartment. I knew that, because I had already sold all my things, I didn't have to worry much about moving. Accepting the fact that I was on the brink of being evicted out of my first apartment was heartbreaking. I wasn't dwelling so much on the fact I was about to be put out on the street, but I was losing something for which I worked so hard. It was only a few months before that I had signed my lease and felt on top of the world, and it was already coming to a depressing end.

Somehow, someway, I found peace in losing my apartment. I embraced the idea that I was going to live in my car. I thought of it as sort of camping. I had never really gone camping, but I tried looking at it from a positive perspective. I was ok losing my apartment; I was ok that I didn't have the best job in the world; the one thing I knew I would keep was my car. My Honda was my baby and I prayed hard to God that no matter what he took me through he would allow me to keep my car. My car was truly one of my greatest accomplishments and I couldn't bear losing it.

On August 1, 2018, at 10:35 AM, I got a call from the leasing office requesting I bring my past due balance up to date or vacate my apartment before they file for eviction. The property manager bargained with me. I didn't want them to go through with the court proceedings and having an eviction on my record, so he gave me the option to move by the next morning and I wouldn't owe anything and they wouldn't file for eviction.

In my closet I'd stashed away the tips I saved once I started delivering pizzas. It was only $200 but I needed nearly $2,000 to pay my apartment complex. The job hunt hadn't stopped and I was working from open to close trying to save up enough money before I was evicted, but I'd run out time.

On the morning of August 2nd, I opened my eyes and let out a deep sigh. Just as the sun started to rise, I moved out of my apartment and into my car.

Shortly after I returned the keys to the leasing office, I drove to work and clocked in. There wasn't much time to dwell on what was happening.

Just four months before, I walked into my apartment thinking it would be my first home to years of memories. I imagined my friends and family visiting and seeing the life I made for myself. I was sure that in due time I would've made friends to have over for drinks and game nights. The future I envisioned for myself was erased by the time I closed my trunk after stuffing it with last of my things. Once again I prayed and hoped for the best, but only the worst followed.

Internally, August 2nd was no different than any other day. My mind still churned with ideas that one day I would look back and see this was worth it all. Somehow I knew this deterrence would only create a better product in me for the future. This shift in dynamics would only drive my work ethic and shape a new perspective on my dedication. I felt insane thanking God for what was going on, but I had no choice. I wasn't depressed. I wasn't heart broken. Most of all, I wasn't lost like I was while in the army. More than ever I was more certain in my capabilities and myself.

Although I wasn't making a lot of money as a delivery driver, I was grateful for my time alone in between each delivery. I constantly thought of grinding harder and harder everyday so I could continue on with my life. It became quality time to think and reconstruct my path to redemption, and without this time alone, I don't know if I would have been able to accept everything that was happening to me and remained focused on persevering.

Accepting the inevitable makes way for a clear thought process. Ignoring the inevitable only creates room for chaos and error to happen. Not wanting to add to the chaos of my life and my finances, I embraced the inevitable.

Tutorial videos on YouTube prepared me for living in a car. To my surprise, there were various videos of people sharing their experience and tips on how to live out of your car. Watching other people embrace and make light of what many others consider ludicrous made this experience feel more like an adventure and less of a defeat. Daily things I took for granted, like brushing my teeth, taking a shower, and eating meals, would all become a challenge. Youtube made this easier with tutorials and video journals of life in your car. I was prepared for this. Nobody, nothing could have made me feel shameful because I knew it was only necessary and temporary.

Usually I was done delivering pizza after midnight during the week and even later on weekends. The roads were clear and traffic lights didn't last nearly as long as during the day. The nighttime had always been thinking about my day to day life. I never focused on the day to day.. Normally, I would take home a pizza and binge-watch episodes of Family Guy until I fell asleep. I blocked a lot out, trying to focus on the future. But this night was much different. Once I clocked out from work the realization of having no home stunned me. I was homeless. The emptiness I felt was heart wrenching.

Leaving work, out of habit I found myself following all the roads that led to my old apartment. I couldn't help but cry when I realized I no longer had keys to an apartment. I had to go find a safe to park where I'd sleep for the rest of the night. Never before had I driven and cried at the same time. This for sure had to be what hitting rock bottom felt like.

    I sat in Walmart's parking lot for about thirty minutes but I couldn't stomach the idea of sleeping in a random parking lot. My pride and dignity didn't want accept the fact of being homeless. My car was loaded with the remainder of my things I hadn't sold. I thought, since I didn't my have to pay rent anymore, I could least afford a room at thirty-five dollars at night. Somehow I talked myself out of living in my car. Living out my car wouldn't be an option until I reached desperate times. I budgeted the daily price of the room and gas. These were my new bills, once I got a second job paying for a room wouldn't be a strain on my pockets."

    I drove to there nearest, cheapest motel I could find. I'd never slept in a motel before. I had stayed in some cheap rooms, but this took the cake for a cheap and sleezy motel. I walked into the bathroom and looked in the shower and my heart sank. It was partly cleaned and the lights didn't work. I didn't trust what I couldn't see so the shower was ruled out. I would've complained, but I didn't expect any other room to be better. I took my blanket from the car and covered the bed so I wouldn't have to come in contact with the stained sheets. There was nothing more I wanted to do more than fall into peaceful slumber and part from everything going on in my world.

CHAPTER 22
Distraction

Should've could've would've's was all I heard from adults as a kid. I should've gone back to school. I could've been a singer one day. Had I listened to my dad, I would've owned my own company by now. I guess it sort of scarred me. I didn't want to have lived thirty or forty plus years on this earth to only talk about what I should've or could've done differently. Because of this, I became painstakingly focused on my future.

I had always tried not to get caught up in senseless things that would distract me from my future goals. Growing up, my mom preached to my brother and I, a thousand times over, to wait before we had kids. "See the world first," she would tell us. Even though I took her words to heart, I never worried about having children at an early age because I don't like girls. Of course, at the time my mom didn't know, so I just went along with the conversation. Therefore there wasn't a big chance of mistakingly getting one of the girls from school pregnant. But by being under my mother's roof, and with her strong religious beliefs, I didn't bother messing around with guys either.

I spent a great deal of time of trying to force myself to be attracted to women, but this only led me to be unhappy and confused. I gave up on trying to find the perfect girl and just zoned in on who I wanted to be when I grew up. It wouldn't be until undergrad where I was free to explore and understand myself sexually. Even then I found it a challenge to fully be whom I was deep down. My mom made me feel astonishingly shameful when she found out I was gay. I naively came out the closet at the end of junior year on social media, thinking it wouldn't get back to my parents because they had a clue what an Instagram was. Regardless, my Mom and Dad found out their son was gay. My dad's respond was underwhelming, but it was my mom's deep Christian beliefs and lack of understanding caused her to lash out at me like never before. I felt like I was living a life that disobeyed God and my mom, the only two people who I really cared to make proud of me. I decided then that life was simpler if I didn't deal with that part of me whatsoever.. I found it more comforting to only think about friends and my career. Friendships grew to be my ultimate idea of companionship. I didn't bother seeking relationships from a partner, only friendships. That way I wasn't living a sinful life and disrespecting my mom's wishes.

My career, on the other hand, was in my control and I allowed it to consume my entire life. I allowed my obsession for a better future to drive my work ethic. Somebody seriously special would have had to come along for me to divide my attention off of my life goals.

Distractions come in many forms: big or small, simple or complicated, and some distractions can cost you your life. I attempted to stay woke enough to avoid the distractions that life often throws at us. However, I'm only human and life's temptations distract even some of the best of us.

I met Chris in mid-June. I believe that love finds you; you can't go looking for it. Not to say what we were in love, but it started to grow there at a super fast pace. He dropped into my life at the worst time possible. He caught me in the middle of my mess but it didn't faze him. Well at first it did, he was disgusted that I quit my job. He didn't quite understand what was going and he didn't realize who he was getting know. I think very highly of myself, not arrogantly, but I'm secured in who am, and eventually who I'll become. When I met Chris I had the biggest crush on him. Something in my mind thought he believed I was nothing more than just a cute face. I liked him a lot from meeting him and I couldn't have thinking so low of me. I still don't know how but, I was able to reconstruct his perception of me. Apparently I did a good job because from that day forth, Chris was practically all mine.

The closer we grew the more I began to be more open and honest with him about what what was going in my life. I was losing everything and I was broker then ever. None of that mattered to him. Just as it didn't ultimately matter to be, we both knew I would come out this predicament Well, at first he was skeptical of my predicament. He offered advice and tried to seem ok with me not having a job at the time but I could tell it bother him. It held us back from getting to know one another other. Had I not given Chris a disclaimer that I was more than the typical dude, he probably would've stopped talking to me after the third or fourth day day. To be honest, I had no business getting to know anybody. I didn't friend, and I certainly didn't have time, energy, space to entertain a potential life interest. I was in the middle of a damn life crisis yet I found time to be up in Chris face almost everyday.

Time with him, from jump, felt so right. He was an escape from all the turmoil I was going through. Our conversations went way deeper than typical questions like, "So, tell me about you?" We shared commonalities and understood each other in a deep, desirable way. When we discussed our aspirations and ideas I felt like I was talking to myself. We saw eye to eye on work ethic and how to move up the totem pole of success. After I explained my vision and what I wanted out of life, he understood me and believed in me more than I did myself. I also knew what he wanted out of life, and slowly I was able to envision him in my future. It was an incredible feeling meeting someone whose upbringing was so far different from my own but yet we held so much in common.

Had it not been for social media, Chris and I probably would've never crossed paths. On top of being from two different states, our childhood were almost polar opposites. While I was caught up in honors classes, performing arts, and student organizations, Chris was gang-banging, throwing up his set, and trapping out the bando". At some point when he was younger he got the name of the gang he was affiliated with tattooed across his stomach. When I met him I thought he was DL (down-low). Like most, at one point he was "in the closet." But now, he's more than confident in who he is. Ultimately it isn't anyone's business but he has stated if anyone feels indifferent about his sexuality he has no problem dealing with them accordingly. I'd never entertained anyone with the similar experience as him. I didn't allow that to depict my feelings for him. I was hung up on how articulate and educated he spoke, to find out he never went to college. I noticed he was well versed, educated and carried himself like a man. Those characteristics stuck out and lured me in. We both worked endlessly. We didn't waste time complaining about working too much, nor did we complain about only seeing each other for only a few hours a day. Nights in the motel started feeling less lonely with his company. I insisted he go home night after night, but he knew how much I hated sleeping in a motel, so he laid with me until I fell asleep before he headed home to his brother's place. The romance was always a plus and kept me at bay. I think being in a halfway decent motel room is probably the complete opposite of vision of romance, but someway he made it feel all right.

One night we sat laying in the bed and we both started feeling biting and itching. I switched rooms that morning because the night before was a slow delivery night and the tips weren't much. Every morning before I left for work I would stop by the front desk to pay for another night in the motel. At the end of the shift, I hadn't made enough to cover the cost of the room but I knew I could make the rest of the money the next day before check out. I made the money and in between deliveries I made a dash to pay for the room. I saw I was too late when I noticed my things sitting outside the room on the sidewalk in clear plastic bags. Furious, I went to the front desk demanding a reason why my things were thrown out on the sidewalk.

I'd been staying there for almost two weeks and I thought there was a mutual understanding that I'd pay for my room everyday, before checkout. It was a pointless argument considering the fact that the damage had been done and I was going to pay for another night regardless of their reasoning. He gave me a key to a new room and apologized, assuring me it wouldn't happen again. I lugged all of my things in the garbage bags to the new room and dashed back to work.

After work Chris came over to the room and as I was telling him about my day and how I got evicted when we started to feel itchy. We tried to ignore it for the simple fact that we thought we were only being paranoid, but as the itching persisted we questioned if the room had bed bugs. Regardless if it was paranoia or actually bed bugs, I couldn't sleep in that room. We took my things, packed my car, and said our goodbyes for the night.

He went home to shower because he couldn't stop itching. By now we both were sure we were being bit and I refused to step foot back in that room. After packing my car, I just tried to fall asleep in the parking lot of the motel.

The itching wouldn't let up and began to really feel like small biting. As soon as I realized I was being bit my heart sank to my stomach because I knew for sure it was bed bugs. As silly as it may sound, I thought bed bugs were a made up thing parents tell their kids. I never knew they were a real thing, nor did I know how much torment they could cause. I tried hard to fall asleep but I could not stop scratching, I couldn't stop itching. I was getting frustrated. I had nowhere else to go. I couldn't have felt more pitiful. I felt so dumb all I could do was cry myself to sleep.

At times life can seem to be so cruel and unkind. In some of the most difficult moments in life we stop ourselves and think, "Why me?" But there's always a counter question we ignore, "Why not me?"

I've always believed that in doing good, good will come to you. I always treated people with the upmost respect and tried not to judge anyone. So why was life treating me so badly? What did I do to deserve all this hardship? When I finally thought things could only get worse, they started to take a turn for the best.

For a long, long time I was alone, but now I had a real relationship with a guy I cared about. We were infatuated with one another. And one day, during a delivery to a new store opening up not too far from where I worked, life really started to put itself back together.

It was a large order, about five or six pizzas. I was eager to take the order because I expected a big tip. I could see the store was a few weeks from opening and there hiring by the signs hanging in the windows. As I was pulling the pizzas out of my car a voice behind me called out, "Hey, you looking for another job?"

Of course I needed a job, but the signs also said they needed associates starting at only nine dollars. I told the lady taking the order, who happened to be the district manager, that I was interested but nine dollars wasn't going to cut it. Then, to my surprise, she said she was looking for a store manager as well as an assistant manager. Intrigued, I took her card to call and set up an interview.

Long story short, I got the job to be the new store manager. I was offered a substantial salary and started almost immediately following the return of my background check. Before the interview I may have tweaked my resume a bit to resemble I had a few years of managerial experience—I was tired of not getting jobs because of not having experience, so I gave myself the experience. I had worked in retail a bit and I knew I was fit to take on this challenge.

Using the same resume, I got the bright idea to apply to more jobs with open management positions. After a few interviews with a gas station in close proximity to my new job, I was hired as an assistant manager. I was now on the come-up; I had not one, not two, but three jobs. I knew within a month's time I would have enough money to move into a new apartment and pick back up where I left off. I didn't want to stop delivering pizza, as it was my only cash flow. It was insane having three jobs when what felt like yesterday I didn't have one. God was showing his favor and grace and I could not have felt more blessed and appreciative.

CHAPTER 23

September

Life was a struggle working three jobs and now I was indefinitely living out of my car. I was done living in the nightmare motel. I wasted my time, threatening to call the health department if I wasn't given a refund. The hotel staff gave me the run around and I grew tired of their games. I called the health department and moved into my car. Brushing my teeth, finding clothes, and even getting dressed was a huge hassle. As for showering, I forgot to return the spare key to my old apartment. I never could muster the courage to shower in the motel, so I tried using the key one late night after work. Luckily the office hadn't changed the locks, so I continued showering in my old apartment until, weeks later, the key stopped working. I thought about sleeping in my old apartment but I feared getting caught and waking up one morning with the police banging on the door.

Once my key stopped working, I got the idea to start a gym membership, that way I had access to a shower. I never thought a twenty-four hour gym would save me me from a hygiene nightmare. I made life work by any way I could. I couldn't waste time wallowing in a pool of self-pity. I thought deliberately and skillfully to survive.

Chris was right by my side along the journey. I enjoyed my time with him but it felt weird deep down. Ultimately, I was homeless and that meant he was talking to a homeless person. I never felt completely comfortable around him. I was constantly reminding myself Chris had a warm bed to sleep every night and I didn't. Deep down I wanted to stop taking to Chris to focus on myself, but he was the only one that listened to every word I said and showed me compassion when I needed it.

Also, I hired him as a stock guy at my store. We just opened and shipments were starting to come in. He needed the extra money and this way we'd be able to spend more time together. I knew never to mix business with pleasure, so we made an effort to be as business-like as possible. Chris needed a second job to save up more money, and I had the power to hire him at my store, so I did.

Everyone I knew thought I was insane for working three jobs. Most days I only had time to work two but there were days I worked all three. In some way I made working eighteen-hour days seem like a breeze, and I owe it all to the army. Physically I was pushed to the max and it was now starting to pay off. Of course I was exhausted from working all the time but I was never unable to deal with it. I knew what it took to get out the predicament I was in: honest, hard work.

After a month of being homeless, I started receiving my first paychecks. Every Friday was a payday and every other Friday was a double payday. Money was no longer an issue. The issue came when I applied for an apartment and was denied because of my credit. Late fees and falling behind on bills ruined my credit. But this was only a small defeat, as I had enough money coming in to catch back up on bills and repair my credit.

I became immune to bad news. My expectations were different now. Whereas before I always had high hopes for people and new challenges in life, now I just go with the flow. Whatever happens, happens. I completely stopped caring. I kept trying but my emotions were detached. It's a somber way of seeing things, but there's a numbing feeling after going through set back after set back.

I simply needed more time to bounce back from everything, and that was ok. I was content with living in my car for the time being. I kept it a secret from everyone except those to which I was extremely close. It was hard trying to convince them I was safe and sane. I wanted to normalize the situation as much as I could.

More and more of my focus turned to Chris. He'd become the center of my attention. We were seeing each other nearly everyday. He was impressed with me by the way I kicked into drive to overcome my circumstances, but I was unimpressed with him by how he started asking for money and looked to me to pay for food and other things when we made plans.

Sure, I was making more money than him, but I was still living in my car. He had a home to sleep in every night and a bathroom down the hall to pee, shower, and brush his teeth. I didn't. Somehow, he found it ok to ask and take from me. Of course I knew he was struggling himself and needed help, but his hand reached far beyond that of help. Most of my money went to paying bills, and I was determined to save the rest. I only spent money feeding us and buying weed. He liked to smoke and I did too. I stopped because I couldn't afford it, but since money was back in my pocket I allowed myself to smoke here and there. But now, I was doing everything for two. I never said anything but it was unsettling knowing the guy I was with was taking from a homeless person.

Getting paid every week made it possible for me to go to Memphis for a trip to New Orleans with my high school friend for her bachelorette party. The trip was inexpensive, and instead of driving I cut the cost of paying for gas by taking a bus to Memphis. From Memphis I would join my friends for a road trip to New Orleans. Usually I'd say I had no business taking a trip anywhere, but it wasn't something I could miss. Robyn, one of my closest high school friends was getting married and she was the first person to get all of our high school friends on a trip out of town together. I needed the escape, and I owed myself the escape. There was so much going on in my life that I needed a break.

During the bus ride to Memphis, I thought a lot about my future. I started second guessing the thing I had going with Chris. In three months time, I'd scraped the bottom of the barrel of desperation and climbed back up into the light of prosperity. All the while he still remained in the same situation in which I met him. I know people move at different paces but it seemed like he was holding me back rather than helping me move forward. Quality time with my day-ones would bring my mind back to focus, back to what was most important and beneficial for my future.

CHAPTER 24
Lord, Why me?

Everyday I make a conscious decision to make today better than yesterday. "Make new mistakes," I tell myself. "Don't make the same mistakes as my parents, don't make the same mistakes I made yesterday, learn from your mistakes and make new ones, it's the only way to grow."

Had it only happened once, I probably wouldn't be writing this book. But it happened twice, and honestly that's two times too many. Days before leaving for Memphis, Chris showed me a new side of him. A darker, angrier side.

I forget where exactly we were headed, but Chris was driving and I was in the passenger seat. Chris was usually the one to drive, because my car was packed with blankets and all of my other things.

It was late in the afternoon. We'd both just gotten off work and the sun was setting. We had just merged on to the expressway. If you know anything about Dallas or Texas traffic, then you know it can be unpredictable and there's construction everywhere. It's a constant battle for your life trying to dodge the crazed drivers and the endless construction cones.

On this particular day Chris added to the mayhem. Nobody pays attention to the speed limit in Texas, so with that being said Chris tried to take off down the freeway once he saw a clear path through traffic. Right when he was about to pass the cars causing the delay, a truck swerved in front of him, cutting him off. In my mind I was thinking "no big deal; this happens all the time here." But in Chris's mind it was ultimate disrespect.

He sped up alongside the truck that cut him him off. A white guy was in the driver's seat, his windows down, and he looked over at us as Chris started shouting at him. He was pointing and cursing at the guy, telling him how he'll beat his ass and how he's got him f***** up. I was pulling on his arm and telling him to stop while keeping an eye on the oncoming traffic. He pushed my hands away and continued yelling out his window at the guy who cut him off. Just when I thought things couldn't get worse, Chris grabbed a nearly empty Gatorade bottle from his cup holder and threw it through the window into the other guy's car. Chris called him a b**** a** n**** one last time and sped off.

As we sped off all I could think about was that guy following us and pulling a gun and lighting us up. Just as the thought crossed my mind I saw the blue expedition in the side of my eye speeding alongside us. Instead of spraying the car with bullets, he gave Chris the middle finger. As Chris tried to react I snatched him back into his seat and yelled, "What the hell is wrong with you?"

I'd never seen somebody's anger get the best of them like that before over something so small. Of course the guy was wrong for cutting us off but we didn't wreck, nor were we even close. Our lives were more in endangered after Chris threw trash at this stranger's car and cursed him out. Call me sheltered or soft, but my life almost flashed before my eyes when I saw him do that—I was floored. I don't and never have acted out of character like that before. I know we are two different people, but nobody I spend my time with and care for is going to act like that. I made myself clear with Chris that behavior like that wasn't going to ever be tolerated. I couldn't and I wouldn't put myself in harm's way, and I certainly wasn't going to let someone else do so for me.

When this transpired, Chris and I had been talking for around four months and I was still learning something new about him every day. Whether it was good or bad, something new and different was constantly surfacing. It's interesting getting to know a person: just when you think you have them figured out they change right before your eyes.

At first, getting to know Chris was a pleasure until he became too dependent on me. I thought hiring him at my job would make things better, but it seemed like I was helping him more than I was helping myself even though I was the one living in a car. At a certain point, I started thinking that it would be better if we both took time apart to focus on ourselves. We were both in poor situations, and bringing two shitty situations together only creates a bigger mess. I wanted more time to focus on myself, and I wanted Chris to have time to better himself as well.

This was all heavy on my mind when I travelled back home to Memphis. Being away both refreshed my mind and confused it. Visiting my family and spending time with my friends made Dallas feel worthless. Something was tugging at me saying move back home, home is where it's at. I knew more people, had more connections. Life would have been easier in Memphis, at least easier than it was in Dallas. In Memphis, I wouldn't be looking for a new parking lot every night for somewhere to sleep. But, in other ways, Dallas felt like a new home. Memphis was old and behind me. I needed to stay in Dallas to prove to myself that all my struggles were worth something. But, then again, I thought of Memphis as an escape route away from Chris, which I then immediately felt badly about. In only four months, he had invested time and effort into me like nobody ever had before, and for that I was willing to keep trying with him. He was willing to change for me, so therefore I was willing to be patient with him.

The second time was the last time. This time was different yet the same. One late afternoon after we work we visited his mom. After we saw her, Chris had to run an errand and I tagged along with him, leaving my car in his mom's driveway. We were heading down the street from his mom's place and there was another car heading towards our direction, but the road we were on was a one-way. The road was pretty wide and Chris could've let the car pass with no problem. Instead of lending a helping hand by telling the gentleman in the car that this road was a one-way, he waited until the car was moments away from crashing into us. Chris blew the horn and yelled out at the car like he hadn't seen it coming all along. It then became clear to me that the other car was an Uber and the driver was just attempting to drop his passenger off. He was clearly lost and confused as to which way to enter the neighborhood.

Chris went off on the man, yelling at him, telling him how he's in the wrong for coming down the one-way. He asserted his point by cursing and calling the man an assortment of names. Just like the last time I tried to defuse the situation by pulling his arm telling him it's ok, to just pull off. And just like before he jerked out of my grip. I tried to be patient with Chris, but when the argument with the Uber driver started to escalate my patience ran out.

Chris enticed a fight by calling the driver a "weak a** b****." He drew the last straw with me with that one. I got out of the car and walked back to his mom's house where my car was parked. I wasn't going to sit around and watch two grown men fight over something so senseless. Just as as the man from the freeway could've had a gun, this Uber driver had every right to have one as well. I wasn't going to wait to find out. I walked back to my car and drove off. I was done with him. But he was far from being done with me.

I made myself very clear the last time. I made it certain he understood that if it happened again I was no longer going to talk to him. To my surprise, instead of asking me to come back, he texted me asking me for my co-worker's number, who were driving to go see in the first place. I wasn't going to give him the number. I didn't want him associating with anyone I knew. I was furious. If he couldn't respect my wishes of not putting my life in danger, I couldn't respect him at all. So I blocked his number after ignoring him, but that didn't stop him from blowing my phone up. I had to block number after number. Instead of letting me go, he harassed me. Sending text after text, calling me out by name, cursing me out, and making empty threats.

At the time, though, the threats didn't feel empty. They felt loaded with anger and regret. I felt like I was dealing with a ticking time bomb, and leaving him sparked the fuse. They say you really don't get to know a person until you've been through something. You really can't see all sides of a person if things are always happy-go-lucky. This side of Chris frightened me. I tried blocking number after number but the calls and texts kept coming. He used every app on social media to contact me. I couldn't keep up with the messages. I tried fighting him off by texting him to leave me alone. I told him there was no hope of me coming back. I suggested he quit his job working with me because it was clear we weren't on good terms anymore. He dismissed my suggestion and insisted I change the work schedule to work outside of my hours so he wouldn't have to see me. I wanted to fire him, but I wasn't sure if I had the authority to fire an employee over personal matters. It was against company policy to hire family members or significant others, as well as a strict no fraternization policy. I needed him to quit but he wouldn't.

The next morning Chris and I were scheduled to open the store. Sunday's were slow, so two person coverage was all that was needed to man the store. I scheduled Chris every Sunday so it could be a day we'd be able to spend together. After what transpired the night before, I hoped he got the picture and didn't come to work, and I called another associate to cover his place. I was relieved when I pulled into the parking and his car wasn't there. I opened the store and was waiting for his replacement, and by this time I was nearly sure Christ wasn't coming, when I saw Chris walk through the front doors an hour and a half late.

Stunned and in disbelief I let him clock in—I didn't know what to do. I hadn't thought about what I'd do if he actually showed up. I let him start working but knew I had to confront him. I let him know his replacement was on the way and when he arrived Chris could go home. I had no choice but to call a replacement because I wasn't sure if he'd show up. I was perfectly fine with him calling my district manager if he had a problem. I told him I'd admit to blocking him and accept all responsibility, but he had to clock out once his replacement came. He took the number and clocked out.

Shortly after leaving an unknown number called me. I feared it was my boss but it was only Chris calling from yet another number asking me to come outside to talk. I hesitantly walked outside to his car while at at the driver's seat with the window rolled down and the piece of paper with my boss' number on it was in his lap.

He said, "This was business and what we had going was personal." He told me I was mixing the two and messing with his money. Coming in the way of his money was a bigger problem than any of the petty stuff we'd fought about before. I could tell he was using his ego to talk at me. I didn't care what he had to say so I just told him do what he had to do. I was done with the situation.

He gave me every right to believe he wanted to get me fired. He said as much, and more, in his long, angry rants to me the night before. This job paid too damn well for it to be taken by a vengeful ex. Instead, I took matters into my own hands and called my district manager to explain the entire situation before Chris called her with a different version of the story. I admitted to going against policy, but I couldn't have anticipated him going nuts over me leaving him. She sympathized with me and instructed me to write a statement. I watered down the seriousness of the matter by saying I hadn't fired him. I was content with him working at the store with one of the assistant managers. Ultimately, I knew he needed the money, and I didn't want to be the guy to take money out of his pockets. I know the feeling of being without money too well to do that to someone else. I wrote the statement with the full intention of letting Chris keep his job.

Nearly a week passed and somehow I felt bad enough to let Chris back into my life. He apologized and assured me that all of the threats he made were just his way of trying to get me back. He promised to change after we had a long heart to heart about expectations. We came together to try to hold on to something we thought was good. We were alike in so many ways and it seemed too unreal to walk away from him so easily. I have always been easily swayed with the right words. I could tell he was remorseful, and my heart was too warm and loving to turn a cold shoulder to his feelings. His apologetic speech turned into a deep discussion about life and the future, which is a trait I admire deeply about him. He's always looking to the future for a better tomorrow, just like me. He maintained a constant thought pattern about what he needed to do in life to yield the results he wanted. Whenever we talked about goals and ideologies, our minds came together like one unified person. When all was said and done, he simply felt like the one for me.

In the middle of our late night talk about life and our relationship, I brought it to Chris's attention that I hated working at the gas station. I had three jobs and it was pointless working a third job that I hated. If it was my only job, I would have had to deal with it, but I had two full-time jobs and a decent part-time gig. So I decided to leave the gas station and search for a different job that I would have liked more, and that's what I did. Just like that, I had a conversation with my manager and avoided the usual two-week grace period before quitting. At the time it felt like a good decision. I thought the next morning I'd start putting in applications to new jobs. If only the next morning wasn't so devastating.

The following morning after quitting my job as assistant manager at the gas station, I felt relived. One less job meant one less responsibility and a few more hours of sleep. I really didn't like that job so I was in great spirits arriving to my store manager job.

The ordeal I experienced with Chris had blown over and I believed he'd never it again. I was really attached him and honestly he was all I had in Dallas. I wanted by my side, I wanted to build something with him until all came crashing to the ground.

I opened the store per usual, the opening cashier was running late. This was no big deal, our mornings started off slow. After completing all the opening procedures, I stepped outside to get some air and look for my employee. Once I made it outside, I could see my district manager parked in her car, almost blending in with the other vehicles in the lot. Seeing her without warning, startled me. Normally she would email or text me saying she was coming by the store. I grew more paranoid pondering why she wasn't parked in front of our store like she always did before. I opened the store alone, which is a big no-no due to safety and liability reasons. I grew anxious by the second, wondering where the hell was my opening cashier. I didn't wanna look bad in front of my district manager, I started to feel like she was watching me and she didn't know that I knew she was watching me.

Eventually my employee arrived and my anxiety was put at ease. I couldn't be mad she was late because I was more relieved she showed up before my DM came inside the store. About 30 minutes to an hour passes and foot traffic in the store picks up. Honestly, I completely forgot my district manager was still out in the parking lot in her car. I carried on with daily business as usual and that's when my district manager entered along with his tall white guy that I had never seen before. My district manager introduced him as the head of Loss Prevention for our company. Once I knew who he was I was excited because I thought he was going to give me tips on cutting down on shrink and possible theft within the store. After she introduced him she took charge of the front end of the store and told me I would be meeting with Mr. LP. I was very cordial and interested in what he had to say until we walked into the back office and he close the door behind him. Initially I thought nothing of it. I thought everything was protocol and he was giving me the rundown about theft but, quickly the conversation took a U-turn and he made aware the real reason why he was visiting my store.

The statement I submitted to my district manager about Chris had come back to hunt me. The Loss Prevention manager took out paperwork and and a pin for me to recall the incident with Chris. Once finished writing, I sat the pen on the table and that's when he let the cat out of the bag. I was being placed on an investigation and while the investigation was being conducted I was suspended from my position, without pay. He gave me the heads up that I violated company policy and I was aware that I violated company policy by admitting guilt in the first statement I submitted. This came out of nowhere I was completely blindsided by the whole ordeal. I had no clue that my termination was in the works. I was devastated because I had to give him my keys and leave the store. Just before I could step away, he reassured me that this wouldn't end in my favor. Fast forward, two days after being humiliated, I got a phone call from my distract manager, explaining the investigation was concluded by terminating my position as store manger. I was fired from violating company policy. The "detailed statement" I gave was supposed to cover my ass but instead my ass got fired!

    I was back at square one with only my delivery job, which wasn't much compared to what I was bringing in with my other jobs. For a second, I thought I was cursed. After leaving the army, my life was a constant struggle, and for the briefest of moments I thought things were going to be better. I thought I was turning my life around, and I saw a sweet road ahead of me. Only for a short time after leaving the army did things get better. Once again I was left with the same questions. Why was this happening to me? God, why me? Why is it one thing after another? What am I doing wrong to cause this for myself?

CHAPTER 25

Resentment

My mom was right. I'm foul in every way and an abomination in God's eyes. I was living a filthy life and God was punishing me for it. Now I understood why my mom lashed out the way she did the night she found out I was gay. She knew God wasn't happy with me and that I would live a life of unhappiness and failure. I thought her words were harmful and cold and solely meant to hurt me, but they were actually words of warning. They had to be. She had to be warning me of God's wrath. For so many years I was filled with happiness and success, but just as soon as I took my focus off what was most important, everything I worked for came crumbling down. Why waste my time displeasing God by going against His will when I can please him by using the gifts and talents that he's given me to live a prosperous life? God is love. But if God is love, then why was I feeling so abandoned and betrayed? This feeling couldn't be from God. God says he'll never leave me and will never forsake me. So why was this happening to me?

In the midst of getting fired I texted Chris to tell him something was going on at work. I told him I was having a meeting with my district manager and an HR rep just before I was blindsided with the news. I called him just after I returned my keys and credentials back over to my boss. He was stunned by the news. He feared he was up next for getting fired, seeing as the statement I wrote was concerned with him. Again, at the time, I thought I was doing the right thing. Chris was a loose cannon and ready to fire at any second, and I didn't want to put my job in jeopardy for an immature relationship with a just as immature boy. Everything I tried to avoid by being proactive blew back in my face.

But, in the end, I could only blame myself for hiring Chris. I knew better. I knew company policy. Chris wanted to take the blame but I couldn't let him. I was an adult who made a conscious decision even knowing the possible consequences.

However, it wasn't actually that easy to accept the blame. In the end, Chris played a huge factor in everything. Had I not been so naive and gullible, I wouldn't have allowed another person to get so close to me where they had the authority or power to ruin my livelihood the way Chris did. I allowed him to get close and he ran amok. I couldn't look at Chris without feeling resentment.

What a price to pay for wanting to help somebody. I thought my track record of doing good would pay off in another form other than friendly fire. For sure, I finally knew I was done with Chris. Even if I wanted to be with him I couldn't now. The very sight of him brought back my feelings of failure and inferiority. It was impossible holding back the tears—I was just weeks away from being stable enough to move into an apartment and pick up where I left off at the start of the summer. No more sleeping in my car, no more driving to the gym just to shower, no more getting dressed in a cramped space, no more worrying about my safety every night in dark parking lots, all this went out the window when I decided to hire Chris because he needed the extra money. Again I asked myself, "Why me?"

CHAPTER 26
All the way home

Saying goodbye to Chris had to have been the hardest thing I'd ever done emotionally. I was torn between choosing me and choosing us. When it was good it was bittersweet. I was infatuated with Chris, mesmerized with everything he did. I was truly happy with him, but he had so much maturing to do. I'm not saying I was perfect or that I didn't have a lot of maturing to do myself. At the end of the day, it simply wasn't about our relationship. It was about choosing me.

I felt like I was giving so much away to be with Chris. I was growing to love him, but it felt wrong to stay. I needed to only focus on myself. I had to walk away from him and it felt like I was ripping his heart out when I told him I would be moving back to Memphis in a matter of days. He couldn't believe it. He didn't want to believe it. I felt like a monster. I felt selfish because I was only thinking of my future and myself. My heart was broken putting Chris through this torment. I couldn't stop crying, he caused so much damage in my life yet I still had deep feelings for him. I told him I would come back for him, but I knew I was lying to him. This was a one-time mistake, taking my eye of the prize cost me dearly. I swore to never fall in love again until I could afford the damage it may cause.

Memphis, TN, a place I've avoided since leaving the army. After all these years, I still knew little about my hometown. My brother and I were sheltered by my mom throughout grade school, and once we graduated we both left Memphis. It had been years since I called this place home, and that's by no accident. Memphis is infamous for its high crime and homicide rates. Memphis is in the top ten of cheapest cities to live in, meaning that job salaries are usually just as low. I avoided Memphis because I never saw it as a place of opportunity. I'm sure there are opportunities, you just need to know the right people.

After I told Chris goodbye, I actually stayed a few days in Dallas. I lingered around the city, living in my car, hoping a job would call me to set up an interview or any other sign from God saying not to move back to Memphis. Amazingly, a company called me to set up an interview after reviewing my resume. This was a corporate position with an admirable salary. I booked a hotel room to properly prepare myself for the interview. That way I could shower, iron, and sleep in an actual bed and get proper rest.

I really thought this was my big break. This had to be God's sign telling me to stay. Instead, the department supervisor believed my experience was too dated and said she was looking for someone with more recent experience. I was extremely let down when I didn't receive a call from her following the interview. I thought for sure that this was it and that I wasn't going to have to crawl back home, poor and broken. But I did just that.

My oldest sister was one of the few people who knew I had been living out my car for the past few months. She told me over and over that I could come to stay with her. I was being stubborn and really believed that I could make it by living in my car until I managed to get my life back afloat. After all that I had been through, I just gave in and told my sister I was coming to Memphis to move in with her.

All the way home to Memphis, I cried. I cried because I felt defeated. I got so distracted trying to be in a relationship even when I knew I had bigger priorities. I loved living in Dallas, I was away from anyone I knew and I loved that. I had my own life away from Memphis, and as soon as I was really doing well for myself I let it slip through my fingers.

I honestly didn't know what I was going to do when I got to Memphis, other than apply for jobs. Nobody other than my sisters and brothers knew I was moving back home. I can't stress how embarrassing I felt going back home. I knew that if anybody found out they would have so many questions—I had hardly told anyone I wasn't in the army anymore, let alone moved to Dallas. My mom didn't even know what was happening. She hadn't called me and I hadn't thought to call her in the midst of everything either. A part of me was somewhat sad that my mom hadn't checked up on me in months, but I never dwelled on it.

On October 24, 2018, I arrived in Memphis, TN. Once I pulled into my sister's apartment complex and parked my car and turned off the engine, I let out a huge sigh. Not a sigh of relief, but a sigh of failure. I unloaded my things and started to take them inside. My new bed was no longer the front and back seat of my car, now it was the floor. My sister didn't have a bed and I started to realize this wasn't even my sister's apartment. It was her husband's brother's apartment and they stayed there because my sister was taking care of her mother-in-law, who suffered from an aneurysm that left one side of her body paralyzed, dementia, bipolar disorder, and Alzheimers. Also, my nephew slept in the room with me. If you're confused about how many people are living in this two-bedroom apartment, that's okay because I was too.

My sister never said she was taking care of her husband's mom. I was under the impression she lived with her husband and just my nephew. I couldn't believe this, but there was nowhere else to go.

CHAPTER 27
What now?

This is not a happy ending. Maybe you read the title and figured I'd overcome my obstacles by the end of the book. If that is the case, then I'm here to disappoint you. Actually, the story gets worse after moving to Memphis. The car I desperately tried to keep, I lost working weeks of moving to Memphis. Its hard to explain the full story but it was devastating to have lost my most prized possession due to confusion with my bank and car dealership.

Now I have literally lost everything. I sold most of my stuff, I lost my apartment, lost all of my jobs, and now my car is gone. My credit is shot and finding a job is now three times harder with no transportation. It felt like I hit rock bottom after leaving Dallas, and now the bottom has given out and I've just been falling even deeper into a dark abyss.

I'm guessing that you've been reading this and thinking to yourself, "You should've never left the army." Part of me might agree with that, but I would still much rather be miserable in civilian life than be miserable in the army.

Needless to say, depression has crept its way back into my life. Crying and sobbing seems like the new norm for me. I know I'm smart, I know I'm capable, so why is this happening to me?

At first, I blamed God. Why did He allow this to happen to me? I prayed long and hard that no matter how bad things got I wouldn't lose my car. Did He not hear my prayer, or did He just ignore me? I wanted God to answer! Understanding was everything to me, and not grasping why I was in this predicament was leaving me uneasy.

This went on until I vividly heard God speak to me. I begged and pleaded, asking God, *Why me?* Almost instantaneously, I was taken back to the moment when I realized I was running out of money. I asked God to prepare me for whatever he had in store for my future. I asked God to humble me in order for me to live out my wildest dreams and, just like that I became at peace with everything. Everything was starting to all make sense to me.

Remember: "No pain, no gain. In order to be something you've gotta go through something." I wasn't right to blame God because he was doing exactly what I asked of him. There's never a reason to be mad at God because He knows all and He knows best. Although this may have been the saddest period I've ever gone through, I'm appreciative of every tear and every experience. I learned so much and grew so much as an individual. The experiences I endured weren't in vain. Mostly important, my skin is thicker and my perspective is broader than its ever been. I see things for what they are and not what they portray to be. There is no gray area in real life. There is black and white, fact and your opinion doesn't matter. Suck it up. Sometimes it's ok throw your pity party, but remember you're the host, responsible for cleaning up the tears as well as the milk that was spilled.

As the days pass, I grow stronger in faith that someday I will be somebody great and influential. I've been forced to understand the path we're on isn't an easy path. It could ordained by God, or it could've be molded out by your parents. Regardless of the path you follow, there WILL be distractions. There WILL be detours. There WILL be potholes along your path, causing flat tires and all types of disarray. Everything I endured has given a connection with someone I may help in the future. Please, don't take my tears and turmoil and feel sorry for me. My story, my experience has liberated my way thinking. I no longer doubt who I am, or who I'm set out to become. Now, instead of getting upset or becoming confused as to why things are happening to me, I now accept what transpired and quickly adapt, learning, so I can maneuver with the new knowledge of a past mistake.

CHAPTER 28
Make New Mistakes

Stop making the same mistakes your mom, dad, sister and bother made. Observe your surroundings and study your past. Learn and understand the obstacles those before you were faced with. Master your family's shortcomings, so they do not also become your downfall.

We all have dreams we want to live out one day. Anything is possible with knowledge and discipline. The mind is the most powerful tool on planet earth. Feed it, use it, and make an effort to learn something new everyday. I lost a lot, but I didn't lose my mind, therefore I am fully capable of overcoming whatever life throws at me going forward.

Trusting the process of life is far easier than giving up or trying to force things to happen in our lives. Had I known I was going to join the army, buy my first car, move to Dallas, sign the lease to my first apartment, lose that apartment, live in a motel then live in my car, lose all my jobs, and be forced to crawl back home to Memphis, I would've tried to prevent each of those mishaps from coming true. But having gone through all of that, I am a better, stronger, wiser individual, and I wouldn't take anything I've endured back.

This book is a long letter to me reminding myself of so many things. Not only to never end up in this predicament ever again, but, most importantly, that no matter how low I fell, no matter how many times the bottom gave out when I thought I reached rock bottom, I always looked to the sky and saw the ledge from where I fell. I stayed determined to climb back to the top and walk on the ground that was destined for me.

Disasters happen every day, but as long as you have your life, able body, and sound mind, anything is possible. It is never too late to go after the thing you love, the dream you want to see come true. Anything is obtainable with discipline and determination. I haven't made it, and I'm far from having it all, but I know one day I will and that's worth the world to me.

I will continue to strive for success. By the time this book is released, I will be in a better place. My life will be enjoyable, and I will have faith and hope again. I don't know how long it will take to get out of my sister's place, but I'm making great efforts to restore my livelihood. Everyday I envision the life I want to live. I drown myself in ideas and ways that, not only will make my life better, but those who cross my path. I pray everyday to be an addition to society.

Yes, my pride is hurt but it's not enough to keep me down. It may be months, it may even be years from now, but I know this story will help somebody overcome a time when giving up seems to be the most logical thing to do. I often ask myself and even friends, *how the hell do you give anyways?* Seriously, picture yourself giving up on life. I can't picture it. There is no imagery, nor fantasy I can conjure up in my mind that portrays a given up Tamarcus. If you're able to picture yourself in this light everything you're doing just change. Feed nothing but positivity into yourself. Because all you have is yourself and that's the only person who ultimately matters.

My hope is that this book will help you see that what you are going through will only help prepare you for your future, that the present is just a small piece of the track to run.

I wrote this book for the senior preparing to graduate college, the son who's battling with his sexuality, the son/daughter who's trying to make it out there on their own with no help from their parents or family, and the potential soldier who's thinking about joining the army as a last resort because his back against the wall. If you are reading this, then this is for you: make new mistakes. Finally remember to go forth, be great by changing your predicament, renewing your mindset, and broadening your perspective.

Thank you

Special Thanks

EVERYONE who told me *no*

Mom & Dad

Grandma Mary and Bettie

Adrian

Robyn

Marissa

Bri

Jared & Jared

Jarvis

Dr. Henderson Dr. Bodie Dr. Murrain

Mrs. Henry and Ms. Patrick

Mr. Broadway

Mrs. Rowell

Ms. Hull

Mrs. Terri

Mr. Brittnum

Mrs. Childress

L.A. Warren and Olivia Goodheart

CPSIA information can be obtained
at www.ICGtesting.com
Printed in the USA
LVHW090855020820
662102LV00009B/74